D1632353

mediterranean
cook

jacqui
small

mediterranean cook

Paul Gayler

photography by David Munns

To the Mediterranean people – whose constant comings and goings have lead to a special sense of hospitality and a desire to please through their food.

MORAY COUNCIL LIBRARIES & INFO.SERVICES

20 11 70 18	
Askews	
641.5918	

First published in 2004 by Jacqui Small,
an imprint of Aurum Press Ltd, 25 Bedford Avenue,
London WC1B 3AT

Text copyright © Paul Gayler 2004
Photography, design and layout copyright
© Jacqui Small 2004

The right of Paul Gayler to be identified as
the Author of this Work has been asserted by him
in accordance with the Copyright, Designs and
Patent Act 1988.

All rights reserved. No part of this book may be
reproduced, stored in a retrieval system, or transmitted,
in any form or by any means electronic, electrostatic,
magnetic tape, mechanical, photocopying, recording
or otherwise, without prior permission in writing of
the Publisher.

Publisher Jacqui Small
Art Director Isobel Gillan
Food Stylist Linda Tubby
Props Stylist Penny Markham
Managing Editor Vicki Vrint
Project Editor Madeline Weston
Additional Text Jane Middleton, Anna Brandenburger
Production Geoff Barlow

British Library Cataloguing-in-Publication Data
A catalogue record for this book is available
from the British Library

ISBN: 1 903221 23 4

Printed and bound in China

contents

introduction

Clustered round the shores of the Mediterranean is a remarkable collection of countries and cultures, from France, Italy, Spain and Morocco in the west to Syria, Lebanon and Israel in the east, and including Greece, Turkey, Tunisia and Albania along the way. So many different races and religions, and such a long history of wars, invasions and migrations. Yet no one who travels through the region can fail to notice a sense of unity, which comes from a common climate and a common way of eating. As Claudia Roden put it in her book, *Mediterranean Cookery*, 'If you belong to any part of the Mediterranean you are never a stranger along its shores.'

The food of the Mediterranean is inseparable from a certain way of life. People still do most of their shopping in daily markets, where they can meet friends and gossip and barter, while choosing from stalls piled high with the freshest seasonal produce. Food is prepared from scratch on a daily basis, and the best cooking is still to be found in the home, where recipes are passed down from generation to generation – or more specifically, as is still usually the case, from mother to daughter. Families eat together, sharing the rituals of the table, and there is a great tradition of hospitality. Even in the poorest of homes, guests are warmly invited in and given the very best to eat and drink. This generosity of spirit has contributed to the special character of the Mediterranean diet – food is for sharing, and for giving pleasure.

AN ENVIABLE CULINARY LEGACY

There is nothing timid about the cooking of the Mediterranean. It is as vibrant and colourful as the climate, as warm and robust as the sun. And as hearty and time-honoured as the many festivals and religious holidays to which it caters throughout the year. Food goes hand in hand with ritual and custom, wherein lovingly-prepared feasts provide the focal point for festive gatherings and specialist dishes add a poignancy in marking each occasion with sublime sustenance.

. The ingredients to hand across the Mediterranean are so good that they require only very simple preparation. When you have such a wealth of lush greens, aromatic herbs and spices, ripe, juicy fruit, and the freshest of fish, the most straightforward cooking treatment will suffice. This respect for the integrity of ingredients explains why you often find remarkably similar dishes from one end of the Mediterranean to another. However, each country will give a dish its own unique accent – for example, in North Africa aubergine purées and salads are enlivened with paprika and cumin, whereas in Italy they are more likely to include fresh herbs, such as mint and basil, or to be combined with capers and anchovies. In this way, a pinch of spice or a scattering of herbs can spell out where you are in the Mediterranean area almost as graphically as consulting a map. Indeed, there are subtle distinctions even when a dish sharing the same name and similar ingredients has been prepared in two unique ways – for example, Greek hummus is traditionally a thicker, rougher paste while hummus made the Lebanese way is a more refined purée: one equally as good as the other, but each dip appeals to different palates.

A REPUTATION FOR BEING RESOURCEFUL

For all its abundance, the food of the Mediterranean has been shaped by poverty. In many areas, the land is rocky and the soil surprisingly poor. Winters can be harsh and bitter, and the flip side of seasonal bounty is long months of shortages. Yet the need for frugality and thrift has given the Mediterranean diet much of its character, and made it an extremely light and healthy way of eating, although also hearty in both bite and flavour. Each ingredient, however small in quantity, provides a good dose of nutrients and this is true with the popular use of nuts both in savoury dishes and in sweet and spiced desserts, to which they add a rich texture. Indeed, there are no limits in a Mediterranean kitchen: marinades comprising oils and fresh herbs are used to pep up the simplest cut of meat, while spices, which are regarded as prize ingredients, are ground at home to lengthen the life of the spice and accentuate its flavour in the food. Wheat and pulses, such as chickpeas, cannellini beans and haricots, form the basis of the diet, together with masses of vegetables. Meat is often reduced to a secondary role, used as not much more than a garnish or a flavouring. When afforded, fish and seafood are cooked using the simplest methods, first marinaded then cooked over a wood fired oven, or oven baked to perfection among tomatoes and garlic.

And dessert is more likely to be fresh fruit than something rich in butter, cream and eggs. Olive oil is the cooking medium of choice, while the unmistakable scent of garlic wafts over the entire Mediterranean region, from the fish stews of southern France and Italy to the tagines of North Africa and the dips and sauces of the Middle East.

KEEP IT SIMPLE AND AUTHENTIC

The simplicity of Mediterranean cuisine is reflected in the basic nature of the equipment used. In some countries, even ovens are not commonplace, and meals for entire families are still produced on a single burner. Spain's classic coastal dish paella is quintessentially a sociable meal, in so far as the paella pans are sized for as many as need feeding, whether 12 or 48 guests are sat at the table! Consequently, most Mediterranean dishes need little in the way of hightech equipment – which is not to say that a food processor or electric blender won't make your task easier. Nevertheless, part of the pleasure of cooking comes from using pieces of equipment that have been employed in the same way for centuries – a mortar and pestle for grinding spices, perhaps, or a terracotta dish for baking stews and casseroles. If this book inspires you to move beyond the basics, as I hope it will, you might also find you want to purchase more specialist items, such as a handcranked pasta machine to make your own pasta, or a couscousière for producing perfect, fluffy couscous.

THIS BOOK

Mediterranean Cook celebrates the generosity of the cooking of the Mediterranean, and more. It preserves the signature of each region's specialist cuisine and imparts a wealth of trusted and traditional techniques together with clear advice on the best preparation of staple, and more unusual, ingredients. This book also embraces a contemporary approach to great tasting food and simple entertaining, providing a wonderful insight into this richly diverse region of the world and the many flavours it brings to our table. Indeed, as you become better acquainted with the inimitable selection of produce sold at your nearest Italian delicatessen or Turkish supermarket, so too will you begin to build a personal repertoire of simple and delicious Mediterranean dishes.

central
mediterranean

central mediterranean
france, italy and spain

The cooking of the central Mediterranean is simple and homely, based on local ingredients in season. But what superb ingredients! Despite the parched, arid nature of much of the land, nowhere else on earth can offer such a bountiful harvest: sun-drenched fruit and vegetables, abundant olives and nuts, sweet-smelling herbs, and iridescent fresh fish. When you have the best ingredients in the world at your disposal, it makes sense to cook them in the simplest possible way so that the flavours speak for themselves. It is this respect for quality and taste that lends sophistication to what is essentially a rustic cuisine.

It could be said that Italy, Spain and the South of France are divided by a common culinary heritage. They share a cuisine of fish soups and stews, mixed vegetable dishes, grilled meats, olive and anchovy pastes, garlic and herb dressings and sauces, yet the preparation of these dishes varies not only from country to country but from village to village, and each region is fiercely proud of its own version. France has its ratatouille, Italy has *caponata*, a sweet and sour stew of aubergines, tomatoes and peppers, the Basque region has *pipérade*, which combines peppers and tomatoes with softly scrambled eggs, and Spain has *escalivada*, a mixture of chargrilled aubergines, peppers and other vegetables. If Provence is renowned for its *bouillabaisse*, a fish stew enriched with a dollop of garlicky *rouille*, then every Italian coastal village has its own version of *zuppa de pesce*, and Spain has *zarzuela*, a Catalan fish stew tinged yellow with saffron. Each country boasts a hearty dish of combined meats: *pot au feu* in France, *bollito misto* in Italy and *olla podrida* in Spain. Perhaps most notable is the use of sauces and pastes based on bread, nuts, garlic, olives and olive oil. Of the nut-thickened sauces, the Italian pesto is perhaps the best known. Spain has *salsa romesco*, made with almonds, *romesco* peppers, tomatoes and garlic, and the Catalan *picada*, a thick paste of garlic, toasted nuts and fried bread. Bread-thickened sauces include the Provençal *aïoli*, a type of mayonnaise in which bread is pounded with garlic and olive oil (sometimes egg yolks replace the bread), and the Spanish version, *allioli*. There is also the Provençal *rouille*, made of garlic, red chillies, bread and oil and served with fish soup. In the South of France *tapenade* blends olives, capers, anchovies and olive oil to a paste, while Italy has many variations on the simpler *pure di olive nere*, or black olive paste.

Olive oil, tomatoes, garlic and herbs are the fundamentals of Mediterranean cooking, forming the basis of most savoury dishes throughout Italy, Spain and the South of France. Olive trees have been cultivated in the Mediterranean area for more than 6,000 years, and their oil is used as its main cooking medium, the basis of sauces and salad dressings, a condiment, and a flavouring in its own right. Extra virgin olive oil is made from the first cold pressing of the olives and has a particularly low acidity, making it the top choice for dressings and uncooked sauces. Ordinary olive oil is a blander, more industrialised product, most suitable for frying.

ABOVE: **1** Lucques Royales olives **2** black olives in oil **3** Niçoise olives **4** balsamic vinegar **5** capers **6** caper berries **7** olive oil **8** membrillo (quince jelly) **9** red smoked paprika **10** ricotta **11** Parmesan cheese
OPPOSITE: **1** peppers **2** wild rocket **3** garlic **4** basil **5** vine tomatoes **6** fennel bulb **7** fennel herb **8** oregano **9** rosemary **10** thyme

Italy produces a huge variety of olive oils, varying from the delicate, pale Ligurian ones to the green and peppery Tuscan oils and the sharp, fruity oils of Apulia and Sicily. Spain, the world's largest producer of olive oil, covers the whole spectrum, from light and fragrant to robust and peppery, while oils from the South of France tend to be sweet and mellow. Olives, too, vary tremendously in style from country to country: the tiny black Niçoise olives of Provence, the large green Ascolana and Cerignola of Italy and the Spanish Manzanilla, to name but a few.

Tomatoes are as much a symbol of the central Mediterranean as olives and garlic, their rich scarlet hue epitomising the colourful and robust cooking of the area. It's impossible to imagine Italy without its

ABOVE: 1 Vialone nano (risotto rice) 2 polenta 3 farro 4 Arborio rice 5 capellini tagliati 6 spaghetti 7 taglierini 8 riccioli 9 tagliatelli 10 troffiette

tomato sauces for pasta and pizza, France without its refreshing tomato salads, or Spain without its gazpacho and sofrito, a slow-cooked mixture of onions, garlic and tomatoes that forms the basis of many dishes. Yet the tomato is a relatively recent addition to the Mediterranean. It was brought back from America by the Spanish in the sixteenth century, only taking a hold on the cuisine in the late

eighteenth century. How lucky that it did – it is well suited to the climate and soil and has a wonderful affinity with olive oil, garlic and herbs.

Despite the relationship between the cooking of this area, each country has a powerful culinary identity of its own. Italian cooking is fundamentally regional, with rice, polenta and dairy produce predominating in the north, pasta, tomatoes and olive oil in the south. Key flavours include basil, oregano, tomatoes, aubergines, peppers, prosciutto, Parmesan and lemon, while Italy's most famous dishes – pasta, pizza and ice cream – have long since conquered the world. In Sicily there is a strong Arab influence, evident in sweet and sour mixtures that include dried fruit, nuts and vinegar.

Spain, too, still bears the imprint of Arab cooking, particularly in its little savoury pies (empanadas) and heavily sweetened pastries, and its use of almonds, citrus fruits, and spices such as cinnamon, coriander, aniseed and saffron. Saffron is most celebrated for its role in paella, which is considered the national dish of Spain. Made with the local short-grain rice, similar in character to Italian risotto rice, paella is a glowing, golden dish that can include poultry, squid, shellfish and chorizo. Yet perhaps Spain is best known for its tapas, that delectable assortment of little savoury dishes that rivals the mezze of the Eastern Mediterranean and the antipasti of Italy.

With its proximity to Spain, the cooking of the Languedoc region of France inevitably has some Spanish overtones. However, its two most famous dishes can claim to be unique – cassoulet, a hearty mixture of beans and meats of which there are several versions and endless disputes about authenticity; and brandade de morue, an unctuous salt cod purée.

The food of Provence combines the best of French and Italian cooking. Pissaladière, a speciality of Nice, is an onion and anchovy tart similar to pizza, while gnocchi are common, and stuffed pasta might be filled with Swiss chard – also, curiously enough, used in a sweet tart. The abundance of vegetables is extraordinary even for the Mediterranean and they are celebrated in dishes such as ratatouille, bagna cauda (an anchovy dipping sauce for crudités) and le grand aïoli, in which aïoli is served with a huge array of raw and cooked vegetables, plus fish, chicken or meat and hard-boiled eggs. Herbes de Provence, a blend of dried thyme, rosemary, marjoram, fennel, oregano and bay, gives the cooking of the region its inimitable character, while basil, anchovies, capers, olives, garlic and orange are also used freely.

knives

Good knives are essential for Mediterranean cooking. Top-quality knives make cooking so much easier and more pleasurable. Sharpness is paramount, but it's important, too, to use the right knife for the job. Choose sturdy knives that you find comfortable to hold, and look for ones where the blade runs through the handle and is joined to it securely with rivets – they are made to last.

1 Parmesan knife A Parmesan knife is shaped rather like a little garden trowel, with a short handle and a rigid, triangular blade. It is used for excavating chunks out of Parmesan cheese, which cannot be sliced neatly because it is too crumbly.

6 Bread knife The best bread knife has a long, serrated blade that can slice through a hard crust without tearing the crumb. It can also be used for cutting cakes and tarts. The serrated blade cannot be sharpened at home but this should rarely be necessary.

2, 3 Cook's knives If you were to have a single knife in the kitchen, a cook's or chef's knife is the one to go for. It is indispensable for dicing and slicing vegetables and herbs, chopping up meat or, using the flat of the blade, crushing garlic and ginger. It has a rigid, heavy blade, ranging from 10–30cm in length, with a gently curved edge. The most useful size is 18–20cm.

4 Filleting knife This straight-edged knife has a slender blade about 12.5–15cm long. It is very flexible, so the blade can work around the contours of the fish bones. It can also be used for skinning fish fillets.

5 Ham knife A ham knife is invaluable for carving a large ham by hand, particularly a prosciutto where thin slices are important. Its narrow, slightly flexible blade is at least 25cm long and enables you to cut slices of even thickness.

knife care

With proper care, good-quality knives should last a lifetime. Store them in a knife block, or in a special canvas wallet or knife case, rather than leaving them loose in a drawer where the blades (and your fingers) might get damaged. Always use a proper board for chopping on, since ceramic surfaces can blunt the blade. Wipe knives clean after use – don't leave them to soak in the washing up bowl – then dry them immediately on a cloth. To keep knives in tiptop condition, sharpen them frequently; it's worth spending a few seconds doing this every time you use them. The best tool for the job is the traditional carbon steel. Hold the steel vertically in one hand and position the knife blade at a 20° angle to it. Move it rapidly across the steel, from the top of the blade to the tip, first on one side, then the other.

7 Mezzaluna This traditional Italian knife has a double handle with a wide, curved blade; it is used in a rocking motion for chopping ingredients finely. It is particularly useful for chopping herbs and garlic to a rough paste – for example, when making *salsa verde*.

crushing garlic

1 Place the garlic clove on a chopping board and cut off the base and tip with a chef's knife.

2 Place the flat of the knife blade on the garlic clove and bash it with your fist, so the clove is lightly crushed and the skin loosens.

3 Remove and discard the skin, then sprinkle a little salt on the garlic. Work the garlic to a rough paste with the tip of the knife blade; the salt helps to break down the garlic.

mandolins

Professional chefs favour mandolins for cutting vegetables into wafer-thin slices or neat julienne strips, and making chips and straw potatoes. Razor-sharp, adjustable blades, either plain or rippled for a crinkle-cut effect, allow you to vary the thickness of the slices. The best mandolins have a safety guard to protect your fingers, and a stand so you don't need to hold it in place. This stainless steel model is top of the range but cheaper wooden versions will do the job too.

making apple lattice slices using a mandolin

1 Set the mandolin on the ruffled blade. Use this on its lower plate, adjust the thickness to about 1.5mm and cut the apples, creating a ridged surface.

2 Twist the apple 90° then slice across the grain to create an open-holed wafer effect.

3 Continue slicing down towards the centre of the apple, turn then repeat with the other sides of the apples.

gaufrette
apple tart

To make these attractive latticed apple wafer tarts you will need a classic French mandolin or slicer. However, they can be produced using simple apple slices cut thinly by hand. Apart from serving them as a light and delicious dessert, they actually make a great base for savoury foods such as pork, fowl or foie gras.

Serves 4
Preparation Time: 55 minutes

Ingredients
550g prepared puff pastry,
    fresh or frozen, defrosted
50g icing sugar, sifted
6 Granny Smith or Golden
    Delicious apples
75g caster sugar
40g unsalted butter
2 tbsp Calvados (apple brandy)

Tools
2 baking sheets
Rolling pin
Fork
Sieve
Vegetable peeler
Mandolin
Heavy based saucepan
Brush

Method
1 Preheat the oven to 190°C/Gas 5. Line a baking sheet with greaseproof paper. Roll out the pastry on lightly floured surface into 25cm square. Place it on the prepared baking sheet, then prick it all over with a fork. Place a second baking sheet on top to weigh it down. Bake for 30 minutes, then remove the top sheet and bake for a further 5 minutes until evenly golden.
2 Sift half the icing sugar evenly over the pastry, return to the oven to lightly caramelise for 1 minute, then repeat on the other side of the pastry.
3 Peel the apples, and slice using a mandolin (see opposite). Discard the core. Arrange the slices on top of the pastry, overlapping by 1cm.
4 Place the caster sugar in a pan and over a high heat, and cook until it becomes golden caramel. Remove from the heat, swirl in the butter and add the Calvados.
5 Brush the caramel all over the apples liberally, then return the apple tart to the oven for 2–3 minutes to glaze, then cut into 4 equal squares and serve.

monkfish osso bucco with citrus gremolata
and farro risotto

Osso Bucco is an Italian dish comprised of thick slices of veal shank, slowly braised with vegetables, aromatics and stock. Here is a recipe I devised some years ago using thick monkfish steaks to replace the veal. The results are excellent. I include a recipe for a barley risotto which replaces the more commonly served Milanese style saffron risotto. You will need to source large monkfish tails for this recipe.

Serves 4
Preparation Time: 45 minutes

Ingredients
2 x 900g–1.35kg large
   monkfish tails,
   skinned, cleaned
2 tbsp plain flour
salt and freshly ground
   black pepper
2 tbsp olive oil
25g unsalted butter
1 garlic clove, crushed
1 onion, finely chopped
1 carrot, cut into very
   small cubes
1 stick celery, cut into
   very small cubes
2 tbsp tomato purée
100ml dry white wine
4 tbsp concentrated
   orange juice
750ml chicken stock
Farro Risotto (see
   opposite), to serve

For the gremolata
3 tbsp chopped fresh
   flat-leaf parsley
peel of 1 small orange
peel of 1 lemon
1 garlic clove, crushed

Tools
Large sharp knife
Cutting board
Large ovenproof
   casserole
Mezzaluna or large
   sharp knife
Bowl

Method
1 Preheat the oven to 200°C/Gas 6. Using a sharp knife, cut the monkfish tail into 5cm thick sections along the fillet and through the centre bone, giving 4 nice portions. Dust the fish in the flour and season with salt and pepper.
2 Heat the oil in a large ovenproof casserole large enough to take the monkfish pieces in one layer. Brown the steaks on both sides, then remove and set aside. Drain off any excess oil.
3 Add the butter and garlic to the pan, throw in the vegetables, and cook over a low heat until the vegetables begin to soften. Add the tomato purée and stir in; cook for 2–3 minutes.
4 Add the wine, orange juice and boil for 5 minutes. Pour on the stock, return to the boil, and season with a little salt and pepper.
5 Return the monkfish steaks to the sauce, cover with a lid, and place in the oven for 20 minutes; alternatively simmer gently on the top of the cooker.
6 Make the gremolata. Using a mezzaluna or chopping knife, coarsely chop the parsley and both fruit peels, then place in a bowl, add the garlic and stir together.
7 Serve the monkfish steaks coated in the sauce, sprinkle a little gremolata over each one, and serve with the *farro* risotto alongside.

using a mezzaluna

The crescent-shaped blade of a mezzaluna means that it can be rolled from side to side without lifting it off the chopping board, making it easy to control. Hold the handles with both hands and move it gently back and forth across the parsley, using a rocking motion.

farro risotto

Farro is a type of hard wheat or barley that has been grown and used in Italy since Roman times. It is usually cooked in soups such as minestrone and other hearty rustic dishes. Pearl barley could be used, but *farro* can be found in Italian delis.

Serves 4
Preparation Time: 25 minutes

Tools	Ingredients	Method
Large saucepan	50g unsalted butter	**1** In a pan, melt half the butter over a moderate heat, add the onion and cook for 2 minutes.
Wooden spoon	1 onion, finely chopped	
Ladle	200g *farro* (Italian barley)	**2** Add the *farro*, cook with the onion for a further minute, then pour on the wine.
	60ml dry white wine	**3** Begin to add the stock, a ladleful at a time, stirring constantly. When the stock is absorbed, add another ladleful.
	450ml chicken stock, hot	
	25g freshly grated Parmesan cheese	**4** Continue adding the stock while cooking until the barley is tender, about 20–25 minutes; stir in the Parmesan and remaining butter to create a creamy texture, season to taste and serve.
	salt and freshly ground black pepper	

tian niçoise

oven baked niçoise vegetables with herbs

A *tian* is a typical Provençal dish, a gratin of layered vegetables, baked in an oval or round glazed earthenware dish or *tian*, from which the recipe gets its name. Practically any sliced vegetable combination can be used. This undoubtedly is one of the tastiest and simplest dishes to prepare and never fails to impress.

Serves 6–8
Preparation Time: 50 minutes–1 hour

Ingredients
5 tbsp virgin olive oil
1 onion, sliced
1 large red pepper,
   halved, seeded, thinly
   sliced
1 garlic clove, crushed
1 large aubergine,
   thinly sliced
salt and freshly ground
   black pepper
450g firm ripe tomatoes
450g small courgettes
1 tsp fresh savory leaves
1 tbsp fresh thyme
   leaves
40g fresh white
   breadcrumbs *(optional)*
10g freshly grated
   Parmesan cheese
   (optional)

Tools
Large frying pan
Large baking dish
Sharp knife
Cutting board

Method
1 Preheat the oven to 190°C/Gas 5. Heat 2 tbsp of the oil in a large frying pan, add the onion and lightly brown; add the sliced pepper, garlic and aubergine, season and cook over a low heat until softened, stirring occasionally, 12–15 minutes.
2 When cooked, scatter the fried vegetables in the bottom of an ovenproof baking dish. Cut the tomatoes and courgettes into 0.5cm thick rounds, then arrange them overlapping in rows on the softened vegetables.
3 Sprinkle the savory and thyme over, season well, then drizzle the remaining olive oil on top and bake for 30–35 minutes.
4 Remove from the oven and serve; alternatively sprinkle the top with the breadcrumbs and Parmesan and return to the oven for a further 10 minutes to form a light crust. Both are delicious!

pasta tools

You can very easily make pasta with just a long rolling pin for rolling out the dough and a sharp knife for cutting it into the required shape. However, there are a few simple and inexpensive tools that are fun to use, give your pasta a more professional appearance, and make the task a little easier.

1 Pasta pan Pasta can be cooked in any large saucepan but a special pasta pan has an inner draining basket, which means you don't have to pour the pasta into a colander once it is done. Instead, simply lift out the perforated basket by its handles and shake to remove excess water. Choose a large pan, so the pasta can move around freely in plenty of boiling water as it cooks: ideally you need at least 4 litres of water for every 500g pasta.

2 Ravioli cutters Individual ravioli cutters are made of aluminium or chrome and have a wooden knob, which makes them easy to hold. They allow you to stamp out perfectly uniform stuffed pasta shapes with an attractive fluted edge. Use the round one for shapes such as *anolini*, *tortellini* and *agnolotti* and the square one for classic ravioli. The cutters can also be used to cut out little biscuits.

3 Ravioli mould This small metal tray looks rather like an ice cube tray, with each indentation having serrated edges. To use, simply lay a thin sheet of fresh pasta on top of it and press gently down into the indentations. Place a little of your chosen filling in each one, then top with another sheet of pasta and roll a small rolling pin (usually sold with the mould) over it. The serrated edges cut and seal the ravioli.

4 Pasta wheel This little gadget is a very useful tool for cutting out squares of stuffed pasta – a knife can be used instead but the pasta wheel seals the dough as it cuts, and gives it a fluted edge. It can also be used for cutting ribbons of pasta such as *pappardelle*, which traditionally has a wavy edge, and for cutting pizza.

pasta machines

Fresh egg pasta is still made regularly in many homes in Italy. Using just two ingredients (flour and eggs), it is not nearly as difficult or time consuming as you might imagine – particularly if you have the right tools for the job. The dough can be mixed by hand or in a food processor, and then rolled out quickly by a hand or electric pasta machine. A hand-cranked pasta machine is not expensive and enables you to produce long, thin sheets of pasta in a matter of minutes. It can be fixed to the work top and the dough is passed between rollers that both knead and roll it. A series of notches makes it possible to move the rollers either closer or further apart. There are also special cutters for producing various ribbon shapes, such as *fettuccine* and *tagliatelle*.

using a pasta machine

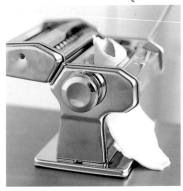 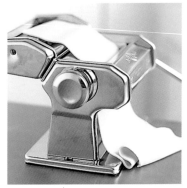 

1 Divide the dough into pieces of about 100g each and flatten slightly. To knead the dough, lightly flour the rollers, put them on their widest setting and feed a piece of dough through. Fold the dough and repeat 4 or 5 times.

2 To roll out the dough, feed it through the machine without folding it, lowering the setting one notch at a time until you reach the required thickness. It is often unnecessary to put the machine on the finest setting.

3 Leave the sheets of dough to rest for about 30 minutes so they dry out slightly. To make ribbon shaped pasta, run the dough through on the required cutter.

pansoti con salsa di noci
stuffed pasta with walnut sauce

Pansoti – meaning 'little tummies' – is a triangular shaped pasta from Liguria, made with flour and wine and filled with five different local wild greens, fresh herbs and flowers, including beetroot leaves, borage flowers, young spinach and wild basil. You can create your own mix. Classically it is made with ricotta cheese, but I prefer a mild goats' cheese, which works well with the slightly sour tasting walnut sauce.

Serves 4
Preparation Time: 50 minutes including resting time for dough

Ingredients

For the pasta
400g plain flour,
    preferably 00 grade
2 tbsp dry white wine
pinch of salt

For the filling
350g mixed herbs and
    flowers (basil, flat-leaf
    parsley, oregano,
    borage)
150g cooked spinach,
    finely chopped
1 egg
2 garlic cloves
150g mild soft goats'
    cheese
50g freshly grated
    Parmesan cheese
salt and freshly ground
    black pepper

For the walnut sauce
2 garlic cloves, crushed
4 tbsp fresh white
    breadcrumbs
125g shelled walnuts
4 tbsp olive oil
25g freshly grated
    Parmesan cheese
4 tbsp soured cream

Tools
2 bowls
Pasta machine or
    rolling pin
Sharp knife
Pastry brush
Pasta wheel
Blender
Large saucepan
Colander

Method

1 Make the filling. Reserve some of the borage flowers for garnish. In a bowl, mix all the remaining filling ingredients together, seasoning to taste.

2 Make the pasta: place the flour on a work surface, make a well in the centre, pour in the wine, add the salt and knead, adding 100ml water to make a smooth dough. Rest the dough for 30 minutes, then cut into 4–6 pieces and roll out by hand or machine, into thin sheets.

3 Using a sharp knife, cut the pasta sheets into 8cm squares.

4 Place a good spoonful of filling in the centre of each square (1), brush the edges with water, then fold over each square in half to form a triangle (2), and press down firmly to seal. Use a crinkled pasta wheel to create a fluted edge to the triangles (3). Place to one side to dry while you make the sauce.

5 Place the garlic, breadcrumbs and walnuts in a blender, whiz to a fine purée, drizzle in the olive oil and add half the Parmesan. Pour into a bowl, stir in the sour cream, and season to taste.

6 Cook the pansoti in plenty of boiling, salted water, drain and transfer to a serving dish. Pour the walnut sauce over, and sprinkle the reserved borage flowers and the remaining Parmesan over before serving.

1

2

3

baby beetroot and ricotta ravioli

I suggest you make this wonderful dish in the late spring and summer, when young beetroots are at their sweetest and most tender. There are numerous ways of making pesto sauce, usually with basil, cheese, pine nuts, garlic and good quality olive oil. This sauce is made with mint and with added broad beans, and makes an interesting alternative to the original. The pesto recipe will make double the amount you need, but will keep well in the refrigerator for up to 4 days.

Serves 4
Preparation Time: 1 hour 15 minutes
including resting time for the pasta dough

making ravioli

1 Lay the pasta sheet over the ravioli mould. Press down gently into the indentations.

2 Fill each compartment with the filling. Brush the exposed dough with a little water.

3 Top with a second sheet of pasta and, using a rolling pin, roll across the mould to seal in the filling. Break up the individual ravioli, place on a tray to dry for 15 minutes.

Ingredients

For the dough

250g plain flour, preferably
  00 grade
pinch of salt
2 eggs and 1 yolk, lightly beaten
1 tbsp virgin olive oil

For the filling

350g raw young beetroots
2 tbsp finely chopped spring
  onions or chives
150g ricotta cheese
50g freshly grated Parmesan
  cheese
salt and freshly ground black
  pepper, ground nutmeg

For the pesto

350g fresh shelled or frozen
  broad beans
1 bunch fresh mint
1 tbsp pine nuts, toasted
2 garlic cloves, crushed
40g freshly grated Parmesan cheese
100ml olive oil
25g pecorino cheese, grated,
  to serve

Tools

2 saucepans
Sharp knife
Mixing bowl
Pasta machine
Blender
Ravioli mould
Pastry brush
Rolling pin
Colander

Method

1 First make the dough: sift the flour and salt on a clean work surface, form it into a mound and make a well in the centre. Pour in the beaten eggs, oil and 1 tbsp water and gradually bring together with your fingers until well combined. Gather the dough into a neat ball and knead for 5 minutes, until smooth and elastic. Cover with clingfilm and let rest for up to 30 minutes.

2 For the filling, cook the beetroots in a large pan of boiling water until tender, refresh in cold water and drain well. Peel them, cut into 1cm cubes and dry on kitchen paper. Place in a bowl with the spring onions, both cheeses and mix lightly together; season with salt, pepper and nutmeg.

3 Cut the pasta into 4–6 pieces and roll out into thin sheets (see page 20).

4 For the pesto, blanch the beans in boiling water for 1 minute, refresh in cold water. Drain, dry, peel off their skins. Setting a quarter of the broad beans aside, place the remaining in a blender with the remaining ingredients, except the oil and pecorino cheese, and whiz until they are finely chopped. With the motor still running, drizzle in the olive oil and season to taste.

5 Make the ravioli (see above) and cook in boiling salted water for 4–5 minutes until *al dente*, then drain well and return to the pan; add the remaining beans, half the pesto and season to taste. Arrange in a serving dish, sprinkle with grated pecorino cheese and serve.

strozzapreti alle tre cipolle

eggless pasta with tomato and spring onions

This recipe for *strozzapreti* with tomato and spring onions comes from my good friend giorgio locatelli – a talented chef with a genuinely warm heart for his beloved Italian cuisine. He says that *strozzapreti* means 'the priest was strangled'. He prepares this for his children as it contains no eggs, however it needs to be quite well sauced in order to keep the pasta moist.

Serves 2
Preparation Time: 2 hours 10 minutes
including resting time

Ingredients

For the pasta
(*strozzapreti*)
500g plain 00 grade flour
pinch of salt
1 tsp olive oil

For the sauce
20g unsalted butter
1 medium red onion,
    cut into julienne strips
1 small white onion, cut
    into julienne strips
3 tbsp virgin olive oil
4 spring onions, green
    and white chopped
    separately
salt and freshly ground
    black pepper
150ml your favourite
    tomato sauce
4 tomatoes, skinned,
    seeded, cut into
    julienne strips
350g prepared
    strozzapreti
    (see above)
4 tbsp chopped parsley
1 garlic clove, crushed
freshly grated Parmesan
    cheese, to serve

Tools

Bowl
Pasta machine
Palette knife
2 small saucepans
2 large saucepans
Colander

Method

1 Mix the pasta ingredients together in a bowl with 200ml warm water, then work into a smooth pliable dough for 2–3 minutes. Using a pasta machine set on a plain roller at 0.5cm thickness, roll out the dough into strips. Cut the sheets in rectangular lengths, about 8cm x 1cm. Using a palette knife, twist the rectangular lengths into small cylinders. Allow to dry for 2 hours.
2 Heat 2 small pans with 10g butter in each. Add the red onion to one, and the white onion to the other, cook over medium heat until soft and translucent.
3 Heat a large pan with 2 tbsp of the olive oil, add the green parts of the spring onion, sweat them for 1 minute, then add both the sweated onions, and season with salt and pepper. Add the tomato sauce, and tomato strips; bring to the boil, then remove from the heat.
4 Cook the pasta in plenty of boiling water until just cooked *al dente*, then drain. Return the sauce to the heat, toss in the cooked pasta, add the parsley and garlic and the remaining olive oil. Serve immediately sprinkled with the white parts of spring onion and some grated Parmesan.

grilling

Stroll round any Mediterranean town and the chances are you will catch the aroma of food being grilled – often in the open air over a simple charcoal or wood fire, which enhances the flavours. It's the perfect way to cook just-caught fish, which needs little other than lemon wedges or a few herbs by way of accompaniment. Lean cuts of meat benefit from a simple marinade, while vegetables should be brushed with oil before grilling.

1 Hinged fish rack These simple wire baskets make cooking delicate whole fish on a grill or barbecue so much easier. Often made to hold several fish, they come in various sizes from sardine size upwards. Oil them lightly before use to prevent the food sticking.

2 Fish slice Not just for use with fish, this handy tool is for turning food during grilling and frying. It is strong, yet flexible enough to slide under food easily. The slots enable excess fat to drain away from the food as you lift it out of the pan or off the grill.

3 Hinged barbecue rack Called a *parilla* in Spain, this flat hinged rack will hold small vegetables or steaks. It prevents smaller items falling through the barbecue grill and makes turning things over very easy. Oil it lightly to prevent the food sticking.

4 Skewers Used throughout the Mediterranean for grilling kebabs, metal skewers conduct heat through the food, ensuring that it cooks quickly and evenly. Flat skewers hold the food in place more securely than round ones. Choose skewers made of sturdy stainless steel and at least 30cm long.

5 Tongs Tongs are invaluable for turning food over on a barbecue or grill. Long-handled ones keep you at a safe distance from the heat of the grill; choose ones that are comfortable, cool to hold and easy to use.

6 Fork A sturdy, two-pronged metal fork can be used for lifting meats from the grill and also for testing whether they are done.

7 Metal grill pan (*la plancha*) The Spanish *plancha* is a metal hotplate for searing food quickly. Portable versions are available with two handles, which make it easy to carry around. Meat, fish and vegetables can all be cooked *a la plancha*, and tapas bars often prepare many of their snacks in this way. Lightly brush your *plancha* with oil before use.

charred beef ribs with cabrales sauce
chuletas con salsa de cabrales

The beef from northern Spain is considered the best in the country as it is reared on excellent grazing lands. *Chuletas* are bone-in rib steaks of beef, meaty and full of flavour – a real treat for big meat eaters. Cabrales cheese is wrapped in chestnut leaves before being matured for up to three months in caves, which gives it its distinct taste. It can be found at any good cheesemonger. I like to serve the steaks on a bed of 'Potataos Parilladas'.

Serves 4
Preparation Time: 25 minutes
plus overnight chilling and marinating

Tools	Ingredients	Method
Blender	4 x 375–450g beef	1 To make the cheese-butter, place the cheese, butter, thyme and mustard in a blender and purée until smooth. Remove to a bowl, stir in the cream and mix well. Scrape out on to a piece of foil, shape into a log and roll up in foil; chill overnight.
Bowl	rib steaks	
Shallow dish	salt and freshly ground	
Metal grill pan (*plancha*)	black pepper	
	100ml olive oil	2 Trim the rib steaks of any excess fat. Place in a dish, season with salt and pepper. Mix the oil and garlic and pour over the steaks and marinate overnight in the refrigerator.
	2 garlic cloves, crushed	
	springs of fresh thyme, to garnish	
		3 Heat the metal grill pan until smoking, then remove the steaks from the oil and grill for 5–6 minutes on each side for rare and 7–8 minutes for medium. Remove and let rest for 2–3 minutes before serving.
	For the cheese-butter	
	150g cabrales cheese	
	100g unsalted butter	4 Remove the butter from the refrigerator, unroll it to remove the foil and cut into slices; place butter slices on top of the steak, garnish with thyme and serve – melting, delicious!
	1 tbsp fresh thyme leaves	
	1 tsp Dijon-style mustard	
	2 tbsp double cream	

potataos parilladas

Tools	Ingredients	Method
Large saucepan	400g large new potatoes	1 Cook the potatoes in boiling, salted water until just tender, allow them to cool. Leaving the skin on, slice them lengthways. Place them on a preheated pan grill (preferably the one just used for the beef) and grill for about 5 minutes each side until coloured and golden. Transfer to a warm bowl.
Metal grill pan (*plancha*)	200g cooked chestnuts	
2 bowls	3 tbsp olive oil	
Whisk	1 clove garlic, crushed	
	juice of ¼ lemon	
	2 tbsp chopped fresh flat-leaf parsley	2 Add the chestnuts to the pan grill and grill lightly for 1–2 minutes.
		3 Meanwhile, whisk the oil, garlic, lemon juice and parsley together to make a dressing. Transfer the chestnuts to the bowl with the potatoes, and toss them in the dressing. Serve with the charred beef ribs.

grilled sardines on catalan bread salad

Tomato rubbed bread (*Pa'amb Tomaquet*) is Catalan's answer to the famous Italian bruschetta. It is primarily eaten as a snack, but is also served at breakfast time. Here I top the bread with sardines. Cook the sardines quickly on a barbecue, set between the bars of a *parilla* (fish rack) over coals: a great barbecue dish for the summer months.

Serves 4
Preparation Time: 30 minutes plus marinating

Method

1 Prepare the vinaigrette by placing the orange juice in a pan, bring to the boil. Place in a bowl, add the vinegars, olive oil, cumin, garlic, season to taste, and mix thoroughly. Place the sardines in a shallow dish, pour over half the vinaigrette and marinate for 2 hours.

2 On the heated charcoal grill, lightly toast the bread on both sides. Squeeze and rub the tomatoes over one side of the toast, leaving flesh and seeds on the surface. Drizzle the oil over, scatter the herbs on top and keep warm.

3 Season the sardine fillets and place them between the lightly greased bars of the *parilla*; place over the hot coals and grill until charred, 2 minutes on each side.

4 Meanwhile, place the salad leaves in a bowl, add the tomatoes, avocado and olives and remaining vinaigrette, toss well together and season to taste.

5 Arrange the toast on a serving plate, top with the grilled sardines, then with the salad, and serve immediately.

Ingredients

300g fresh thick sardine
  fillets
4 slices crusty bread,
  about 2cm thick
2 large very ripe
  tomatoes
3 tbsp Spanish virgin
  olive oil
8 fresh basil leaves,
  chopped
1 tsp fresh thyme leaves
75g assorted salad leaves
6 cherry tomatoes,
  halved
½ avocado, cut into
  chunks
8 black olives, pitted

For the vinaigrette

4 tbsp fresh orange juice
1 tbsp white wine
  vinegar
½ tbsp sherry vinegar
5 tbsp Spanish olive oil
1 tsp cumin seeds,
  toasted, ground
1 garlic clove, crushed
salt and freshly ground
  black pepper

Tools

Small saucepan
2 bowls
Whisk
Shallow dish
Charcoal grill
Fish rack (*parilla*)

moulds

Although elaborate desserts are not eaten every day in the central Mediterranean, something special will always be prepared for festivals and holidays. In France, it might be a rich creamy charlotte or a spectacular glazed fruit tart, made from local apricots, plums or cherries, while Italy is renowned for its sorbets and ice-creams, often moulded in special tins. Spain has a tradition of rich caramel custards, based on egg yolks and cream and baked in large tins or individual dishes.

1 Charlotte mould A traditional aluminium charlotte mould is bucket shaped, with sloping sides and two little handles to make it easier to turn out. The classic charlotte is made by lining the lightly buttered mould with ladyfinger biscuits, which may need to be trimmed to fit, then filling it with a rich, egg custard or mousse, sometimes using gelatine as a setting agent. The mould can also be used for soufflés, puddings, ice-creams and jellies.

2 Dariole moulds With their tall, sloping sides, dariole moulds can be used to make elegant individual servings. They are used for desserts such as baked custards, mousses, crème caramel and individual sponge puddings. Since they are made of metal – usually stainless steel or aluminium – they react quickly when heat is applied, making it easy to turn them out.

3 Ramekins Varying from 100–250ml in capacity, porcelain ramekin dishes have straight, smooth sides and a decoratively ridged exterior. Besides making individual savoury or sweet soufflés, they can be used for baked custards, such as *crema Catalana*, a type of *crème brûlée*.

4 Tart tins These are available in a range of shapes and sizes. Loose-bottomed ones with fluted edges are both attractive and practical. Deep tins are suitable for sweet or savoury tarts with a fairly substantial filling, such as a quiche or a custard-based tart. Shallow tins, about 2–3cm deep, work well for delicate fruit tarts. For individual servings, you can buy little tartlet tins, about 8–12cm in diameter. Always preheat a baking sheet in the oven and place the tart tin on it: this helps to set the crust.

5 Oval dariole Oval dariole moulds make an interesting alternative to the more commonly available round ones. They are particularly effective used for cold savoury mousses and aspics, of the sort often seen in traditional French *traiteurs* (delicatessens).

6 Copper crown mould This mould has a distinctive sculptured shape and can be used for cakes and fruit mixtures. Tiny ones such as this make appealing individual portions. The funnel in the centre helps to ensure that the heat reaches all parts of the cake quickly, and when turned out, the hollow can be filled with whipped cream or fruit. This shape also makes an ideal mould for mousses or ice-cream. To turn an ice-cream out of the mould, dip it in a bowl of lukewarm water for about 30 seconds, and place a chilled serving plate on top. Invert both and lift off the mould.

candied fennel tart

tarte au fennel confit

This unusual combination of sweet fennel and buttery pastry is a real masterpiece. In Provence fennel is a much loved and prized vegetable, and it is remarkable how well it suits this dessert preparation, with its liquorice like flavours. jean claude guillon is executive chef of the Grand Hotel du Cap Ferrat in Monte Carlo, known for its superb cuisine. Jean Claude normally serves his fennel tart with ice cream, highly perfumed with star anise, a wonderful combination. Try this recipe: I am sure you will discover a new favourite yourself.

Serves 4
Preparation Time: I hour 20 minutes plus overnight chilling

The day before
I Prepare the custard. In a small saucepan, scald the milk with the vanilla over medium heat. Strain if a vanilla pod has been used and set aside. In a medium sized bowl, whisk the eggs, add the sugar, beat again, then mix in the flour. Pour the egg mixture into the top of a double boiler. Heat gently over simmering water. Gradually stir in the warm milk, and cook, stirring constantly, until the custard just reaches boiling point, remove from the heat, cover and chill overnight.

Method
2 Preheat the oven to 240°C/Gas 9. In a saucepan, mix the sugar with 400ml water, stir to dissolve and heat slowly to boiling point, Simmer uncovered and without stirring for 10 minutes. Gradually add the fennel, stirring. Cook at a slow boil until the fennel is translucent and candied, about 25 minutes. Remove from the syrup with a slotted spoon and set aside.
3 Roll out the pastry to 0.3cm thick, then cut into 4 x 12.5cm circles using a cookie cutter. Use the pasty circles to line 4 lightly greased 10cm tartlet tins or rings with only a small raised rim.
4 Spread the chilled custard on each shallow pastry round. Arrange the crushed fennel on top in an even layer. Bake for 15 minutes. Sprinkle with icing sugar, then return to the oven for 2–3 minutes longer. Garnish with fennel sprigs and serve with ice cream.

Ingredients
350g granulated sugar
450g Florence fennel,
    tough outer leaves
    removed, cut into
    Icm dice
300g prepared fresh or
    frozen puff pastry
    (defrosted if frozen)
50g icing sugar
100ml thick custard
    (see below) or store
    bought

For the custard
(makes 750ml)
400ml milk
I vanilla pod, split or
    I tsp vanilla essence
2 eggs and I yolk
100g caster sugar
3 tbsp plain flour

fresh fennel sprigs, to
    garnish

Tools
2 small pans
Bowl
Whisk
Double boiling pan
Wooden spoon
Slotted spoon
Rolling pin
Cookie cutter
4 x 10cm tartlet tins
    or rings

charlotte aux marrons
chestnut charlotte

Limousin is the richest chestnut growing area of France. This light yet rich tasting dessert seems to have disappeared from the French tables in favour of less elaborate creations. However it is a must for this book, and I include it in celebration of *haute cuisine Française.*

Serves 6–8
Preparation Time: 30 minutes
plus overnight chilling

Ingredients
75g unsalted butter,
  softened
350g unsweetened
  chestnut purée
225g caster sugar
5 tbsp dark rum
3 × leaves gelatine
  (soaked in water for
  5 minutes)
300ml double cream
18 boudoir sponge
  fingers
8 marrons glacés,
  chocolate flakes,
  to decorate
icing sugar, to dust
double cream, to serve

Tools
1 large, 1 medium bowl
Wooden spoon
2 saucepans
1.5 litre charlotte mould

Method
1 In a large bowl, beat the butter and chestnut purée together until light and creamy in texture. In a pan bring 175g of the sugar with 4 tbsp of water slowly to the boil, until the sugar has dissolved and forms a light syrup. Boil until the syrup thickens for 5 minutes, remove and cool.

2 Add the syrup into the chestnut mixture, add the rum, gelatine leaves and beat well together; set aside to cool. Whip the cream and lightly fold into the cool chestnut mixture, set aside.

3 Place the remaining sugar in another pan with 1 tbsp water and bring to the boil slowly to dissolve the sugar. Raise the heat and allow the sugar to caramelise to a light golden brown then remove from the heat.

4 One at a time, dip the sides of the boudoir fingers into the sugar. Stand each one upright to line the sides of a 1.5 litre charlotte mould. The caramel will bind them together, but should not touch the mould itself. Cover the bottom of the mould with any remaining fingers or trimmings. Drizzle any remaining caramel over.

5 Carefully spoon in the chestnut mix and level at the top; cover and refrigerate overnight.

6 Turn out the mould to serve, decorate with chocolate flakes and marrons glacés. Dust with icing sugar and serve with lashings of double cream!

spanish earthenware pots

Virtually every Mediterranean country has its own version of the traditional earthenware cooking pot. A *cazuela*, also known as a *cassola*, is the Spanish version and is available in a variety of sizes. They are glazed inside, which makes them easy to clean, and retain the heat extremely well. Use on the hob (with care) and in the oven, for cooking rice, soups and stews, or fish and meat. Avoid sudden changes of temperature and always heat them up gradually, otherwise they might crack.

1 Puchero Like the casserole, and the French *tian*, a *puchero* refers to both the cooking vessel and the stew that is cooked in it. A traditional *puchero* is made of cast iron or earthenware with two handles, and narrows at the neck.

2 Small cazuelas About 15–25cm in diameter, these *cazuelas* are a good all-purpose size. Use them for side dishes, or for cooking and serving individual portions of seafood, such as sizzling prawns with garlic. The terracotta finish holds the heat well, enabling food to be cooked with a minimum of liquid and little extra fat.

3 Cazuelitas Tiny *cazuelas* such as these don't have handles and are only about 2.5cm deep. They are great for individual tapas portions, or as serving dishes for nibbles such as olives and nuts. You could also use them for egg dishes or for rice puddings and *crema Catalana*.

4, 5 Large cazuelas The oval *cazuela* (4) has an attractive rustic finish on the outside but the interior retains the traditional glaze. It is the ideal shape for cooking fish or poultry. The round dish (5) is deeper, making it more suitable for rice or vegetable dishes. All *cazuelas* should be cured before their initial use by immersing in cold water for several hours. They can then be used in the oven or on the hob although, to be on the safe side, you might prefer to place a heat-diffusing mat underneath. After use, simply wash the *cazuelas* by hand and dry.

tapas

Nothing draws inspiration from Spain's most pleasant gastronomic pastimes – the ritual of tapas. Local *tascas* (or bars) celebrate the pre-dinner hours with a vast and alluring array of small tasty snacks, accompanied by a *chato* or glass or wine or sherry. The lively flavours of the tapas pique the appetite, while the tender morsels provide substance between the midday meal and customary late Spanish dinner.

I include four of my favourite tapas, adapted from the vast repertoire Spain offers; they may be prepared in advance, leaving you to indulge in perhaps another delightful Spanish pastime, the afternoon siesta, before your guests arrive.

bacalao frito with escalivada

Salt cod (*bacalao*) is a staple of Spanish cuisine, especially in the Basque region. Today it is found in trendy restaurants serving *neuvo cocina*, new Spanish cuisine. As a general guide, I find the larger the fish, the better the quality. It should always be slightly pliable and not stiff as a board. Clean salt cod in running water, then soak for 48 hours in clean water, changing the water two or three times, then remove all skin and bones. Prepare this wonderful recipe, crisply fried in batter, served with *escalivada* (toasted vegetables).

Serves 4
Preparation Time: 50 minutes including 30 minutes for resting batter

Ingredients
1 onion, grated
1 garlic clove, crushed
1 tbsp chopped fresh
   flat-leaf parsley
pinch of powdered
   saffron
1 tbsp olive oil
6 tbsp plain flour
¼ tsp baking soda
vegetable oil for deep
   frying
200g desalted, salt cod
   skinless, cut into 1cm
   thick strips
Allioli (garlic sauce), to
   serve (see page 50)

For the *escalivada*
3 tbsp Spanish olive oil
1 aubergine, seeded
1 red pepper, halved,
   seeded
1 tbsp chopped fresh
   oregano
salt and freshly ground
   black pepper

Tools
Large bowl
Ridged grill pan
Sharp knife
Deep fat fryer
Slotted spoon

Method
1 In a bowl mix the grated onion, garlic, parsley and saffron; add the olive oil, flour and baking soda and enough cold water to form a batter consistency. Leave to stand for 30 minutes.
2 Meanwhile, prepare the *escalivada*: heat a ridged grill with 1 tbsp of the oil, when hot add the aubergine and pepper and grill for 8–10 minutes until tender and charred all over. Remove to a cutting board and cool, before cutting into 1cm strips. Place in a dish, cover with the remaining oil and sprinkle the oregano over and season to taste.
3 Heat the vegetable oil to 180°C, then dip the cod pieces into the batter, working in batches, then carefully fry them until golden, about 1½–2 minutes, turning them during cooking. Remove with a slotted spoon on to kitchen paper to drain off the excess fat.
4 Serve the fritters on the charred vegetables, accompanied with Allioli sauce.

alcachofas alinas (dressed artichokes)

Artichokes can be a fiddle to prepare and a little time consuming, however, the tiny baby artichokes now readily available are much easier to prepare and need less trimming and cleaning. This recipe is one I had in a tapas bar in Barcelona, it was quite hard trying to get the recipe from the owner, who did not speak one word of English. However patience prevailed, and here it is. Most Spanish vegetable recipes include the cooking liquid as a sauce.

Serves 4
Preparation Time: 20 minutes

Ingredients
8 baby artichokes
1 lemon, halved
100ml white wine
½ tsp cumin seeds
pinch of powdered
   saffron
3 garlic cloves
50g ground almonds,
   toasted
½ tsp dried chilli flakes
1 tbsp tomato purée
5 tbsp virgin olive oil
2 plum tomatoes, finely
   chopped

Tools
Sharp knife
Cutting board
Saucepan
Mortar and pestle
   or blender

Method
1 Trim the artichokes and remove any tough outer leaves, either leave them whole, or half or quarter them, depending on size. Rub the cut surfaces all over with the cut lemon. Squeeze the juice from the lemon.
2 In a pan, boil the wine with 300ml water, add lemon juice, and boil for 15 minutes. Meanwhile, in a mortar crush the cumin seeds with the saffron and garlic, and add to the cooking liquid with the almonds and dried chilli flakes.
3 Add the tomato purée and oil and finally add the artichokes and cook until tender, about 12–15 minutes.
4 Remove from the heat, and let cool in the liquid. When ready to serve, add the chopped tomatoes and serve at room temperature.

calamari in black vinaigrette

Calamari, more commonly known as squid, are caught in large numbers in the Mediterranean, and are extremely popular in tapas bars all over Spain. They are extremely quick to cook, either grilled, deep fried, stuffed and braised, and are highly nutritious. Although I suggest always buying fresh shellfish, calamari are one of the few shellfish that doesn't seem to suffer from freezing, your fishmonger will clean them for you ready for cooking. Tiny plastic sachets of squid ink are important for this dish, and can be purchased in many fishmongers or fish markets.

Serves 4 tapas servings
Preparation Time: 5 minutes

Ingredients
300g small or medium squid (calamari)
3 tbsp virgin olive oil (preferably Spanish)
1 small onion, sliced
1 sachet of squid ink
1 tbsp white wine vinegar
1 garlic clove, peeled, sliced
1 small red chilli, seeded, very finely chopped
1 tbsp chopped spring onions or chives

Tools
Sharp knife
Serrated knife
Saucepan
Slotted spoon
Bowl
Frying pan

Method
1 Cut the body of the calamari open to make one flat piece, keep the tentacles in their bunches, and remove the eyes and mouth.
2 Using a serrated knife, score the inner side of the flattened body with parallel lines 1cm apart, then the same the other way to make criss cross hatching. Cut into 1cm thick strips.
3 Heat 1 tbsp of the oil in a pan, add the onion and fry gently until soft, about 3–4 minutes. Add the ink, 6 tbsp of water and let it boil on a low heat for 5 minutes. Remove the onion with a slotted spoon into a bowl, place on one side.
4 Heat a frying pan with some of the remaining oil, and when very hot, add the squid strips, and cook for 2 minutes only. Remove with a spoon and add to the onion in the bowl. Pour the vinegar over and toss together.
5 Heat the remaining oil left in the pan, and fry the garlic slices until golden, add the chilli, then add to the bowl with any cooking oil in the pan and leave to cool. Toss the calamari vinaigrette and serve sprinkled with the spring onion.

stuffed potato tortilla

Tortillas or Spanish omelettes are one of the most popular forms of tapas or appetiser to any meal. The Spanish love eggs, preparing them in all manner of delicious ways, from baking them with peppers, peas and ham, frying them with paprika and cheese, or simply hardboiled and stuffed with tuna and chives. Unlike the British, they rarely consume eggs for breakfast, preferring them as a lunchtime or evening food. Some Spanish cooks cook the potatoes with no colour, others prefer them browned, as I do.

Serves 4–6 tapas servings
Preparation Time: 30 minutes

Ingredients
175ml virgin olive oil
750g potatoes, peeled, thinly sliced
1 onion, sliced
5 eggs, beaten
salt and freshly ground black pepper
100g shelled and skinned broad beans
75g chorizo sausage, thinly sliced

Tools
Heavy based frying pan
Large bowl
2 large plates
Cutting board
Serrated knife

Method
1 Heat the oil in a heavy based 20cm frying pan, or non-stick pan. Add the potatoes and onion and cook over a moderate heat until the potatoes are golden and tender, stirring frequently, 15–20 minutes.
2 Drain off the excess oil from the pan, and place the potatoes and onion in a large bowl. Add the beaten eggs, and season well with salt and pepper; when cooled, add the broad beans.
3 Return the oil to the pan, and when hot, pour in the egg, potato and bean mixture. Cook over a low heat for 10 minutes until almost cooked through. Carefully slide the tortilla on to a large plate. Invert another plate over the tortilla and turn the plate upside down. Slide the tortilla base back to the pan, and cook the reverse side.
4 Slide the golden tortilla on to a cutting board, leave to cool.
5 Heat the pan once again with no oil, add the chorizo slices and quickly fry until golden and slightly crispy, remove.
6 With a serrated knife, cut the whole tortilla in half horizontally and fill with the crispy chorizo, replace the top section. Cut into neat wedges or squares and serve at room temperature.

crema catalana

This recipe, one of Spain's simplest, yet greatest desserts, comes courtesy of my good friend, luis irizar. After many years working in Spain's greatest restaurants, Luis now runs his own catering school in San Sebastián, giving a new generation of Spanish cooks his enviable knowledge and years of experience.

Serves 4–6
Preparation Time: 15 minutes
plus 1 hour chilling

Ingredients
6 egg yolks
150g caster sugar
25g cornflour
1 litre full fat milk
1 cinnamon stick,
  broken in half
peel of ½ lemon
3 tbsp brown sugar
  to glaze

Method
1 In a bowl, whisk together the egg yolks and the sugar.
2 In another bowl, mix together the cornflour with 3 tbsp of the milk.
3 Boil the remaining milk in a pan with the cinnamon stick and lemon peel, remove from the heat and leave to infuse for 2–3 minutes.
4 Strain the milk, then pour the milk over the egg yolk mixture, whisking continuously; mix well, add the diluted cornflour, then return to the pan and slowly return to the boil.
5 Allow to cool before pouring the creamy mixture into 4 individual glasses; sprinkle with brown sugar and burn with a blow torch until caramelised, chill and serve.

Tools
2 bowls
Whisk
Saucepan
Strainer
Blow torch gun

hake with butifarra, peppers and chard

Hake is the most loved fish all over Spain, especially on the Galician coast. It is a firm, moist white fish, ideal for many preparations from poaching, frying to baking, to grilling, a real treat at any time. I prefer to use the larger fish which yield lovely thick steaks. You could substitute cod for this dish. *Butifarra negra* the famous spicy black pudding sausage, that also comes in a white variety, but any black pudding will do the job.

Serves 4
Preparation Time: 25 minutes

Tools
Large saucepan
Colander
Large casserole
Fish slice

Ingredients
150g Swiss chard, stalks removed, chopped
4 x 200g hake steaks on the bone
flour for coating
salt and freshly ground black pepper
4 tbsp Spanish olive oil
4 garlic cloves, crushed
2 red peppers, seeded, cut into chunks
100g *butifarra negra*, cut into 1cm slices
100ml dry white wine
250ml fish stock
3 hard boiled eggs, quartered
Allioli sauce, to serve (see page 50) *(optional)*

Method
1 Blanch the chard in boiling salted water for 2–3 minutes, strain in a colander, leave to drain.
2 Coat the hake steaks in the flour, mixed with a little salt and pepper.
3 Heat the oil in a suitable casserole, large enough to take the steaks laying flat. Add the steaks and quickly brown the fish on both sides, then remove.
4 Add the garlic, peppers and *butifarra* to the casserole and cook gently for 4–5 minutes until the peppers begin to soften; remove to one side.
5 Return the fish to the casserole, and immediately pour on the wine, do not stir, but shake the casserole, add the stock and form a sauce while the fish cooks.
6 Return the garlic, peppers and *butifarra* to the casserole, add the chopped chard, and season with salt and pepper. The total cooking time for the fish is 10–12 minutes. Finally garnish with the quartered eggs and serve with Allioli sauce, if you like.

roasting tins

Throughout the Mediterranean there is a tradition of roasting meats with herbs and other aromatics. Modern technology means that there is now a superb range of options for roasting tins, ranging from non-stick cast iron to enamel or anodized aluminium. One advantage these have over traditional materials is that they are easier to clean. Choose a heavy-duty roasting tin that will not buckle in the heat of the oven and can be used on the hob, too.

1 Stainless steel roasting tin The sides of this roasting tin are deep enough to prevent the fat splattering but low enough for direct oven heat to reach the food. Handles make it easy to lift out of the oven. A tin this size is ideal for smaller joints of meat or for a chicken.

2 Ceramic baking dish Ceramic baking dishes absorb the heat well. The wide, shallow shape means that the food has a large surface area and forms a crust easily – ideal for baked pasta dishes such as lasagne and for gratins. The dish is attractive enough to take to the table and serve the food directly from it.

3 Enamel roasting tin This tin is large enough to hold a big joint of meat, such as a shoulder of lamb or a rib of beef. The dark colour absorbs the heat easily, while the smooth surface is very easy to clean. In one corner there is a lip for pouring off fat and juices after roasting.

---

roasted red mullet with bay leaf, fennel and olives

The *Provençaux* love nothing better than freshly caught red mullet (rouget), whether in soups or cooked flavoured with other local ingredients, such as lemon and olives. The bay leaves add a wonderful flavour to the fish and the olive oil should be Provençal too of course. Roasting whole fish is one of the best ways to attain a moist and fragrant fish with crisp skin.

Serves 4
Preparation Time: 35 minutes

Tools
Sharp knife
Large roasting tin

Tip
Occasionally I serve this roast fish with a herb butter made by simply blending fennel, capers, watercress and unsalted butter in a blender, and chilling in the refrigerator. Serve in a separate dish to dress the fish.

Method

1 With a sharp knife, make 3 slashes on each mullet down to the bone, then stud each incision with a fresh bay leaf.

2 Place the mullet on a lightly greased large roasting tin. Season the fish cavities with salt, pepper, then fill each with tomatoes, half the lemon slices, the olives, garlic, and the fennel and basil leaves.

3 Drizzle the olive oil over, season again all over the fish with salt and pepper.

4 Roast the fish until the skin is crisp and the fish is cooked and tender, about 20 minutes in all. Allow the fish to rest for 2–3 minutes, arrange the remaining lemon slices on the fish and serve.

Ingredients

4 x 475g red mullet,
  gutted and scaled

12 fresh bay leaves

salt and freshly ground
  black pepper

4 firm tomatoes,
  thickly sliced

1 lemon, sliced

100g black Niçoise
  olives

4 garlic cloves, peeled,
  sliced

1 bunch fresh fennel

12 fresh basil leaves

100ml virgin olive oil

pans

Good saucepans are expensive but they make a huge difference to the success of your cooking and should last a lifetime. The essential features are a material that conducts heat evenly, such as aluminium or copper, and a thick, heavy base that does not scorch or buckle. Other points to look out for are lids that fit tightly and well-made handles that are securely attached to the pan. Ovenproof handles are a bonus if you want to transfer your pan from hob to oven.

1 Large saucepan These pans are made of stainless steel, which is non-reactive, so it doesn't taint the food. It is also rustproof, extremely hard wearing, and easy to clean. The larger saucepan has tall sides, making it suitable for long cooking as the liquid does not evaporate quickly.

2 Small saucepan The stainless-steel smaller saucepan is more suited to making sauces or cooking small quantities of food. Stainless steel is not in itself a good heat conductor so choose pans which have a layer of aluminium or copper in the base.

3 Sauté pans Also made of stainless steel, these classic sauté pans have a wide, base and straight, shallow sides, making them suitable for brisk frying. The low sides allow liquid to evaporate rapidly, while the heavy, flat base ensures even browning. Some sauté pans come with a lid, making them more versatile.

4 Crêpe pan Sweet and savoury crêpes are popular throughout France, often sold on street corners from mobile stalls. These are cooked on a large flat griddle, but in the home a special crêpe pan is used. It is small (about 17–20cm in diameter) and has lower sides than a frying pan so the crêpe can be turned easily.

5 Paellera This is the pan to buy if you are serious about cooking Spain's most famous dish, the paella. It should be at least 35cm in diameter, with short, sloping sides and a flat base, and has two handles. The wide base is ideal for cooking rice, since it allows the liquid to evaporate easily and helps the rice to form a light crust.

seafood fideos
noodle and seafood paella

Eating paella in Spain is a way of life – this one, made with short thin noodles (*fideos*) instead of rice, originated in the Alicantine town of Gandia, south of Valencia. According to maría josé sevilla, whose recipe this is, *fideos* were brought to Spain by the Arabs. In her wonderful books, María brings out the culture and traditions of Spanish cooking like no other writer.

Serve 6
Preparation time: 55 minutes

Ingredients
75ml olive oil
300g monkfish, boneless, cut into chunks
300g squid, cleaned, bodies cut into rings plus tentacles
2 garlic cloves, peeled, chopped
1 large tomato, skinned, finely chopped
¼ tsp paprika or *pimentón*
pinch of salt
6 raw prawns (preferably Dublin Bay prawns), in the shell
12 raw king tiger prawns, in the shell
12 fresh clams in shell, cleaned
12 mussels, cooked and removed from shells
300g *fideos* noodles or spaghetti, in 2.5cm lengths

For the stock
2 tbsp olive oil
2 onions, roughly chopped
6 garlic cloves, peeled
1 large tomato, chopped
500g fish bones

For the *picada*
2 garlic cloves, peeled
3 tbsp chopped fresh parsley

Tools
Large saucepan
Paella pan (*paellera*)
Mortar and pestle
Ovenproof casserole

Method
1 For the stock, place the olive oil in a pan, add the onions, garlic, tomato and fish bones. Pour in 2.5 litres of water and bring to the boil, simmer for about 15 minutes, strain and reserve the hot stock
2 Preheat the oven to 180°C/Gas 4. Heat the olive oil in a paella pan (*paellera*) and cook the monkfish and the squid for 5 minutes. Add the garlic, tomato, paprika, a little salt, and cook gently for 5 minutes. Add the prawns, clams, mussels and simmer for 3–4 minutes. Add the pasta, then pour in the fish stock. Bring to the boil, then simmer for about 10 minutes.
3 Meanwhile make the *picada* by pounding the garlic and parsley in a mortar and pestle.
4 Add the *picada* to the paella pan. If your oven is big enough, place the paella pan in the oven and cook for 5 minutes to slightly crisp the surface. If not transfer to a large ovenproof casserole and finish cooking in the oven.

1   2   3

Ingredients

For the *socca*

200g chickpea flour
   (gram flour)
100g plain flour
1 large egg
125ml double cream
2 tbsp extra virgin olive
   oil, plus extra for
   the pan

For the filling

2 bunches chives
5 tbsp extra virgin
   olive oil
2 garlic cloves, lightly
   crushed with a knife
4 bunches rocket, tough
   stems removed,
   washed, dried
2 bunches watercress,
   tough stems removed,
   washed and dried
salt and freshly ground
   black pepper
2 bunches basil, leaves
   only, washed and dried

Tools

Small pan
Strainer
Large frying pan
Plate
Sieve
Large bowl
Whisk
Crêpe or omelette pan

Method

1 Make the filling. Bring a small pan of salted water to the boil, toss in the chives, and boil for a minute. Drain the chives in a strainer, refresh in cold water, and dry well on kitchen paper.

2 Place the olive oil and garlic in a large frying pan over a medium heat. When you catch a healthy whiff of garlic, remove and discard the garlic cloves. Add the rocket, watercress, season, and cook, stirring until the greens have wilted and released their liquid, about 2–3 minutes. Add the basil, cook for 30 seconds to wilt, then drain off the liquid, transfer to a plate and cool. When cool, roughly chop the greens and the chives, season, and set aside.

3 For the *socca*, sift the flours together in a large bowl, add salt and pepper. Make a well in the centre of the flour. Drop the egg into the well *(1)*, then gently whisk into the flour. Very slowly add 625ml warm water, then the cream, whisking gently all the while until smooth, and the consistency of cream (if the batter is too thick, add a little more water)*(2)*.

4 When ready to cook the pancakes, whisk the oil into the batter.

5 Warm a 20cm crêpe (pancake) or omelette pan, over a medium heat until it is hot, then drizzle in a tiny bit of olive oil. Pour in just enough batter to coat the bottom of the pan with a thin even layer, about 4–5 tbsp. Cook the pancake until it bubbles, flip it over *(3)*, and cook for a minute or so on the other side. Prepare all the pancakes in the same way. Stack them under a kitchen towel as you make them (the cooked pancakes may be kept at room temperature for an hour or two, or made the night before and refrigerated).

6 To serve, preheat the oven to 200°C/Gas 6. Spread a thin layer of filling over each pancake and fold the pancake in quarters or alternatively roll up. Reheat the pancakes in the oven for 3 minutes. A well flavoured tomato sauce goes well with these *socca* for vegetarians.

socca stuffed with peppery greens

Socca is a soft chickpea pancake, a popular food sold on the French Riviera. It is a traditional morning snack, prepared on large trays sometimes up to 60cm in diameter and cooked in a large wood-burning ovens like the ones used for baking pizzas or *tortas* in the streets of old Nice. The following recipe by daniel boulud make socca-like pancakes, made of chickpea flour and filled with peppery greens, including rocket, basil and watercress, utterly delicious. Daniel is one of New York's, and the world's most respected chefs. This dish makes an ideal vegetarian dish or an accompaniment for roasted chicken or beef.

Serves 8 (makes 16 pancakes)
Preparation Time: 20 minutes

pizza tools

Pizza is the perfect example of a dish that is greater than the sum of its parts. It consists of just bread dough and a simple topping, yet when it is skillfully prepared and baked in a wood-fired oven, a kind of alchemy takes place, producing one of the world's most popular foods. Very few of us can bake pizza in a wood-fired oven but it's still immensely satisfying to make it at home. A few simple pieces of equipment will make the task all the more pleasurable.

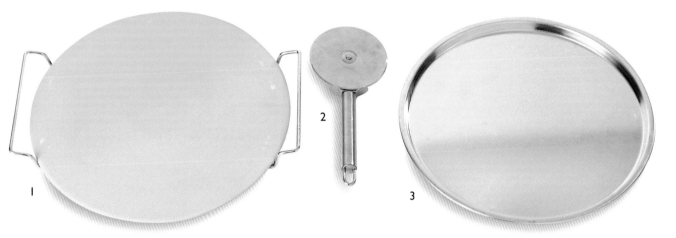

1 Pizza bakestone This thick, unglazed, round terracotta slab helps give pizza a light, chewy crust similar to one baked in an authentic wood-fired brick oven. Heat your bakestone in a hot oven for 20–30 minutes before sliding a prepared pizza on to it. It can also be used for baking bread, particularly flatbreads such as focaccia.

2 Pizza cutter Made of stainless steel, a pizza cutter is a small, rotating wheel with a handle, which cuts cleanly through cooked pizza. It is a much more efficient way of dividing it into portions than with a knife.

3 Pizza pan Pizza pans are round, flat metal baking tins, often with a perforated base to allow the air to circulate, which results in a crisper crust. The darker it is, the better the crust will be, as the heat will be conducted more efficiently. Preheat a baking sheet in the oven, then put the uncooked pizza in the pizza pan and place it directly on the hot baking sheet.

focaccia with fig and prosciutto

Focaccia is one of my favourite breads, simple to prepare and tasty, a staple of Italian cuisine. It can be flavoured with all manner of ingredients from olives to herbs to chilli! It is also great used as a base for a sort of pizza. This recipe is from one of America's brightest chefs, todd english. Here Todd tops the dough with a heavenly marriage of fresh figs and prosciutto with rosemary.

Makes 4 focaccia
Preparation Time: 2 hours
40 minutes including rising time

Ingredients

For the dough
350g plain flour
25g wholemeal flour
2 tsp fresh yeast, crumbled
2 tsp coarse salt
2 tsp sugar
2 tsp extra virgin olive oil
425ml lukewarm water (37–38°C)

For the topping
1 tbsp extra virgin olive oil
½ tsp kosher salt
6 figs, quartered
2 tbsp honey
1 tbsp chopped fresh rosemary
  leaves or 1 tsp dried rosemary
8 thin slices prosciutto

Tools

Food processor/mixer
with dough hook
Tray
Tea cloth
Baking stone
or baking tray

Method

1 To make the dough, combine the flours, yeast, salt and sugar in the bowl of a mixer fitted with a dough hook. While the mixer is running, gradually add the oil and water. Knead on low speed until the dough is firm and smooth, about 10 minutes. Divide the dough into 4 balls (about 215g each). Place on a tray, let them rise in a warm place, covered with a warm damp cloth, until doubled in bulk, 1–2 hours.

2 Preheat the oven to 200°C/Gas 6. Place a baking stone in the oven. Prepare the focaccia by placing each ball of dough on a lightly floured surface and punch down with your fingertips into a 18–20cm disk so that you end up with a dimpled surface.

3 Drizzle the surfaces with oil, then evenly distribute the salt, figs, honey and rosemary over the surface. Place the focaccia on the baking stone in the oven and bake until golden brown, 15–20 minutes. Top with prosciutto slices before serving.

artichoke and ricotta torta
thin artichoke and ricotta pie

A *torta* is the name of an Italian pie, usually a savoury one, consisting of a vegetable based filling wrapped in a thin dough and baked in a wood-fired oven like a pizza or on an open fire. Savoury pie-making dates back to Egyptian and Roman times, and they are made all over Italy to the present day. Here is an adaptation of one I had in Liguria – rustic, just in its simplest form.

Serves 6–8
Preparation Time: 2 hours 40 minutes
including proving

Ingredients

For the pastry dough
250g plain flour, plus
   extra for dusting
½ tsp salt
3 tbsp virgin olive oil

For the filling
2 tbsp olive oil, plus
   extra for brushing
1 onion, finely chopped
150g ricotta cheese, well
   drained
75g Parmesan Reggiano
   cheese, finely grated
4 large cooked artichoke
   bottoms, diced
5 hard boiled eggs,
   shelled, chopped
1 bunch fresh marjoram,
   chopped
½ bunch fresh flat-leaf
   parsley, chopped
1 egg yolk
salt and freshly ground
   black pepper, ground
   nutmeg

Tools
2 large bowls
Small frying pan
33cm pizza pan
Rolling pin
Pastry brush
Pizza cutter

Method

1 In a large bowl mix together the flour and salt. Make a well in the centre, add the oil and add 100ml of cold water, a little at a time, mixing with your hands until the dough just holds together.

2 Knead the dough until smooth and elastic, then shape into a ball, return to the bowl, cover and place in the refrigerator for 2 hours.

3 For the filling, heat the oil in a small frying pan, add the onion, cook for 2–3 minutes then place in a bowl; add the ricotta, Parmesan, artichoke, chopped eggs and herbs. Add the egg yolk, season to taste with salt, pepper and nutmeg and leave to cool.

4 Preheat the oven to 190°C/Gas 5. Lightly oil and flour a 33cm round pizza pan. Divide the dough into two and roll out the bottom crust to cover the pizza pan; cut off any overhang with a knife. Top with the filling leaving a 2.5cm border of crust exposed around the edge (1).

5 Roll out the top crust and trim to a 30cm circle; place on top of the filling. Wet the edge of the bottom crust, then fold in over the top and crimp to seal (2). Use a fork to pierce several holes all over the *torta* to allow the steam to escape. Gently brush the top of the *torta* all over with a little olive oil.

6 Bake in the oven until crispy and golden, about 35 minutes and cut into 6 wedges using a pizza cutter or sharp knife to serve.

Tip
Many other fillings may be used using the same principle, for example spinach and potato, or wild mushroom and ricotta.

1

2

small tools

Small tools such as the ones pictured here tend to be simple and inexpensive yet they make many kitchen tasks a great deal easier. Most of them have proved their worth over centuries of use, and it is particularly satisfying to know that you are preparing ingredients in a time-honoured way – grinding whole spices in a mortar and pestle, for example, or whisking egg whites to a stiff, white froth with a balloon whisk. Look after these simple tools and they will last a lifetime.

1 Olive oil bottle and spout This elegant bottle is a classic French design. Made from white china, it protects the oil from the light. The stopper is a stainless steel spout set in cork, which seals the bottle and makes pouring easy and drip free.

2 Lemon squeezer A variation on the classic glass lemon squeezer, this stoneware version is a very effective way of extracting juice. When a halved lemon is pressed down and twisted over the ridged dome, the juice collects in the base of the squeezer, while the pips are prevented from falling into it by the little pointed teeth.

3 Birch whisk Make of slender, stiff branches, a birch whisk is used for mixing liquids and light ingredients together.

4 Balloon whisk The balloon shape and thin, flexible wires allow maximum amounts of air to be incorporated when whisking egg whites or cream. Balloon whisks come in a range of sizes, so always use one appropriate to the quantity you are whisking. Stainless steel is the best choice as it is easiest to clean and will not rust.

5 Flat whisk A flat whisk has flat looped wires and is useful for blending small amounts together or lightly whisking a single egg yolk.

6 Sauce whisk This small, flat whisk has a flexible coil that helps to make sauces such as béchamel and hollandaise perfectly smooth and lump free. It is shaped so that it can reach into all corners of the pan, and the flat, rigid handle is easy to hold.

7 Reamer For centuries the wooden reamer has been used to extract the juice from lemons and oranges. For a simple, cheap and effective tool, it is still hard to beat. To use, cut the fruit in half and, holding it over a bowl, push the reamer into it, twisting to extract all the juice and crush the pulp.

8 Citrus zester This is an invaluable tool for removing thin strips of citrus zest without cutting into the bitter white pith below. It has a small, blunt blade with five sharp-edged holes in it. Simply scrape it down the citrus fruit to remove all the zest in neat, fine strips.

9 Pitter A pitter is a neat way of removing stones from olives and cherries. The most readily available type looks like a small pair of tongs, with a ring-shaped holder for the cherry or olive at one end and a prong at the other end to push out the stone.

10 Corer The rigid, hollow, cylindrical blade of the corer is sharp enough to cut through firm fruit such as apples and pears and the right length to remove the core in one piece. To use one, hold the fruit steady on a board and push the corer straight down through the centre. Twist slightly to remove; it should bring the entire core out cleanly with it.

11 Melon baller Shaped like a small scoop, this allows you to serve melon in small, neat balls rather than dicing it into cubes. It is also useful for scooping out the core from apples and pears.

12 Mortar and pestle Mortars and pestles come in a vast range of sizes. The one shown here is ideal for grinding a small amount of spices, or for crushing herbs, garlic and nuts – when making pesto, for example. It is ceramic, but they are also available in stone, wood and marble. The inside of the bowl and the base of the pestle should be slightly abrasive, to provide friction and help the grinding process.

13 Garlic press A sturdy garlic press can crush whole, unpeeled garlic cloves, pushing the flesh through the tiny holes in the base and leaving the skin behind. To use, place a garlic clove in the cavity and bring the top handle down, so the garlic is forced through the press. Metal presses are generally more effective than cheaper, lightweight plastic ones.

14 Churros mould (*churrera*) Breakfast in Spain wouldn't be the same without *churros*, crisp doughnuts for dunking into coffee or chocolate. And *churros* wouldn't be the same without a *churrera* – a special syringe through which the batter is extruded directly into hot oil. It comes with a choice of discs to slot into the base, to make doughnuts of different shapes.

salsa verde
italian green sauce

I recently decided to explore the classic *salsa verde* because I had seen so many ways to prepare it and thought it was time to put the record straight. So here is the result: a recipe dating back to 1652! Traditionally it is served with *bollito misto* (boiled meats), but is great with fish, vegetable and pasta dishes.

Serves 8–10
Preparation Time: 10 minutes

Method
1 Place the garlic cloves in the mortar and crush them, add the herbs and anchovy, and crush to a pulp.
2 Add the egg, mustard, gherkins and capers and crush to a purée-like consistency.
3 Finally add the vinegar and slowly drizzle in the oil to form a semi fluid sauce.
4 Season to taste with salt and pepper and serve.

Ingredients
3 garlic cloves, peeled
1 bunch fresh flat-leaf parsley, leaves only
1 bunch fresh basil, leaves only
4 anchovy fillets
1 hard boiled egg
½ tsp Dijon mustard
50g sweet dill pickled gherkins
50g salted capers
2 tbsp white wine vinegar
6 tbsp virgin olive oil
salt and freshly ground black pepper

Tools
Mortar and pestle or blender

allioli sauce
garlic sauce

Allioli is the simplest of sauces, just garlic and oil! Nowadays, eggs are added to stabalize the sauce, however this is optional, and whichever method you choose, it is delicious with all manner of grilled meats, fish and shellfish.

Ingredients
6 large garlic cloves, peeled and chopped
1 tsp coarse salt
250ml good quality virgin olive oil
a little lemon juice
3 egg yolks (optional)

Tools
Mortar and pestle or small blender

Makes 300ml
Preparation Time: 5 minutes

Method
1 Place the garlic and salt in the mortar, and crush with the pestle to form a purée. If using, add the egg yolks one by one.
2 Add the olive oil drop by drop to form an emulsion, finish with lemon juice to taste.

raw vegetables with provençal anchovy dressing
l'anchoïade de salade des légumes

One cannot write a book on the food of the Mediterranean without including a recipe for *anchoïade*, the strong flavoured sauce for anchovy lovers, offset with the pungency of vinegar and garlic – a real winner. It is great served with raw vegetables in this recipe from one of France's greatest chefs, my good friend roger vergé. Roger is an amazing man and his culinary passion for Provençal cuisine shines through in his superb food

Makes 250ml
Preparation Time: 15 minutes

Ingredients

1 can anchovy fillets, soaked in milk for 1 hour, dried
200ml extra virgin olive oil
2 garlic cloves, crushed
1½ tsp fresh thyme (wild if possible)
1 tbsp chopped fresh basil
1 tbsp Dijon mustard
1½ tbsp wine vinegar
freshly ground black pepper

selection of vegetables, such as steamed baby artichokes, fresh green, red, and yellow peppers, cucumber, fennel, carrots, cauliflower, radishes, celery, mushrooms, cherry tomatoes, all cut into strips or bite-size pieces for dipping

Tools
Blender
Spatula

Method

1 In a blender, place the anchovies, olive oil, garlic, thyme, basil, mustard and vinegar, whiz to a purée, season with pepper.

2 Transfer to a bowl that can be taken to the table for guests to dip the raw vegetables in.

Alternative Method

Roger also recommends another method: combine the anchovies with 3 tbsp of the oil in a pan and warm it gently on the heat. Scrape the anchovies into a food mill placed over a large bowl, add garlic, thyme and basil, run through the mill. Scrape off any of the mixture that clings to the bottom of the mill and add to the bowl, whisk in the mustard, vinegar, pepper and then add the remaining oil until incorporated.

churros with almond milk ice cream, and raisin caramel

Churros are simply Spanish-style doughnuts and are sold and eaten throughout the day – bought from local bakers, sold in street cafés, always accompanied by a cup of hot chocolate for dunking. They are shaped with a special forcing nozzle called a *churrera*, which, unless you visit Spain, may be difficult to find. However a piping bag with a star nozzle does the trick. Here, I prepare them as a dessert served with almond ice cream and sherry caramel, why not? A recipe not for the diet conscious may I add!

Serves 4–6
Preparation Time: 30 minutes
plus 4 hours or overnight chilling

Tools
Blender
2 bowls
Strainer
2 large saucepans
Whisk
Ice cream machine

Wooden spoon
Deep fat fryer or large frying pan
Nylon piping bag with star nozzle or *churrera*
Slotted spoon
Small saucepan

1

2

3

4

Ingredients

5 tbsp vegetable oil
1 tbsp ground cinnamon
zest of 1 lemon
200g plain flour, sifted
½ tsp salt
1 egg
vegetable oil for deep
   frying
4 tbsp caster sugar

For the ice cream

100g whole blanched
   almonds
100ml full fat milk
350ml cream
6 egg yolks
100g caster sugar

For the raisin caramel

250g caster sugar
2 tbsp sherry
50g raisins

Method

1 First make the almond ice cream: place the almonds in a blender with 150ml water and the milk, whiz to a smooth purée. Pour into a bowl, leave overnight or up to 4 hours, then strain.

2 Heat the almond-flavoured milk and the cream to almost boiling. Beat the egg yolks in a bowl with the sugar until light and fluffy. Gradually whisk the almond milk into the egg yolk mixture, return to the pan, stir constantly over a low heat until the mixture thickens and coats the back of a spoon: it is important not to allow it to boil or it will curdle. Remove and cool, before freezing in an ice cream machine according to the manufacturer's instructions.

3 For the *churros*, boil together 300ml water and the oil with half the cinnamon and the lemon zest. Add the flour and salt, and beat well with a wooden spoon over a low heat until it leaves the sides of the pan clean; when cool beat in the egg. Heat the vegetable oil in a deep fat fryer or large frying pan to 180°C.

4 Spoon the mixture into a nylon piping bag fitted with a large star nozzle or *churrera*. Pipe the mixture into the oil *(1)* and cut off in 7.5 lengths *(2)*, a few at a time, and cook until golden, turning them once. Remove with a slotted spoon *(3)* and drain on kitchen paper. Mix together the remaining cinnamon and the sugar and sprinkle over the *churros (4)*.

5 Make the caramel, heat a small saucepan on a high heat, add the sugar and cook until it becomes golden caramel. Stir in the sherry and raisins and cook for a further 2 minutes. Arrange the *churros* on a serving plate, serve with the ice cream and a little of the raisin caramel.

clafouti limousin
batter cake with black cherries

Clafouti is the name given to this classic French dessert, both simple to prepare and utterly delicious. Traditionally, clafouti is made with unpitted, wild cherries, giving it a slightly almond-like flavour. Other fruits such as pears, apricots and apples are excellent prepared in the same way.

Serves 4
Preparation Time: 50 minutes

Method
1 Preheat the oven to 200°C/Gas 6. Place the cherries in a bowl, add the kirsch and lemon zest, and set aside.
2 In a pan, bring the cream, milk, almond essence and half the sugar to the boil. Place the eggs and remaining sugar in a bowl, whisk until creamy and light in texture. Add the flour and salt, whisk until smooth. Whisk in the boiled cream and milk, beat to amalgamate.
3 Butter the inside of an ovenproof dish well. Add the cherries, then pour the batter mixture over the cherries.
4 Cook in the oven for 20–25 minutes. Remove and cool until warm, dust with icing sugar and serve.

Note
Vanilla sugar is made by burying fresh vanilla pods, halved and split, in a jar of caster sugar which is left to stand for at least 4 days before use.

Ingredients
500g black cherries, pitted
4 tbsp kirsch liqueur
¼ tsp freshly grated lemon zest
150ml whipping cream
100ml full fat milk
¼ tsp almond essence
120g vanilla sugar
4 eggs
20g plain flour
pinch of salt
25g unsalted butter for greasing
icing sugar for dusting

Tools
2 bowls
Saucepan
Whisk
25cm ovenproof dish

balkans

balkans
greece, cyprus, turkey and albania

Set at the crossroads of East and West, the Balkan countries benefit from a serendipitous blend of influences on their cuisine. It combines the freshness and simplicity of the Western Mediterranean with the rich, exotic flavours of the East. Perhaps no region of Europe has a more chequered past than the Balkans, with its long history of invasions, religious struggles, emigration and violent coups, and this has had a huge impact on its cooking. Conquering armies came and went, leaving behind their culinary legacy, while centuries of trading meant that a fruitful culinary interchange took place.

The varying climate and terrain of the Balkans are reflected in the food that is produced and eaten. Down in the sun-drenched coastal regions the preparation and cooking is kept to a minimum with simply grilled fish or meat a staple favourite. Up in the mountains where the temperature is cooler the more elaborate and time-consuming dishes have evolved. With such a long and varied history much of the food has developed an essence all of its own. Many of the dishes have borrowed spices, cooking methods or even cooking vessels from other nations who have come to settle here. The warm sun and clear air allow the fruits and vegetables to grow in abundance with strong distinctive flavours and recipes have come from the simple combinations of these ingredients.

The cooking of each country has its own distinctive character but there is also a strong common thread in terms of both ingredients and techniques. Lamb, or very often mutton, is the meat of choice, used to make stews, roasts, grills and a huge variety of kebabs and meatballs. Dairy produce is a staple, particularly yogurt, which is often made from ewes' milk rather than cows', resulting in a rich, tangy flavour. And each country prides itself on its huge repertoire of vegetable recipes.

Turkey, with its imperial past, has perhaps had the biggest impact on the cooking of the area. In many ways it has acted as a catalyst, imposing its culinary style on the nations it conquered, while assimilating and reinterpreting the dishes of its vanquished neighbours. *Meze*, that glorious array of little dishes, originated in Turkey and can be found in many other Balkan countries too. A variety of hot and cold appetisers are beautifully arranged on trays, and might include pickles, salads, purées (such as taramasalata or hummus), stuffed vegetables, little savoury pies, sausages and egg dishes.

Börek, another Turkish classic, are also common in Greece and Albania – savoury pastries made from leaf or flaky pastry in a variety of shapes and sizes, from triangles and squares to cigar-shapes and tight, snake-like coils. Fillings vary from lamb and chicken

to soft cheese, feta and spinach, often enlivened with fragrant herbs such as cinnamon, dill, mint and coriander. In Greece and Cyprus, larger pies are made, too, such as *tiropeta*, filled with eggs, feta and soft cheese, and *spanokopita*, which combines feta with spinach and dill. Stuffed vine leaves are as well known in Greece as they are in Turkey, yet the name,

ABOVE: **1** walnuts **2** pistachio nuts **3** bulghur wheat **4** dates **5** raisins **6** prunes **7** filo pastry **8** dried apricots **9** kadaif pastry
OPPOSITE: **1** vine leaves **2** oregano **3** mint **4** grapes **5** aubergine **6** feta cheese **7** thyme **8** Greek yogurt **9** fig

dolma or *dolmades*, comes from a Turkish word meaning 'to stuff'. An indispensable part of any *meze* table, they are made with meat and/or rice and sometimes pine nuts and currants, flavoured with tomato, and spices and herbs such as cinnamon, mint, parsley or dill.

Turkey is renowned for its meat dishes, and in particular for its meatballs, or *köfte*, and kebabs. Shish kebabs are cooked on skewers, and can

ABOVE: 1 olive oil 2 vinegar 3 rosewater 4 cinnamon 5 black peppercorns 6 coriander seeds 7 allspice

consist of either large chunks of meat or very finely chopped meat that has been worked to a paste with flavourings such as onion, spices and herbs, then moulded round the skewers by hand. Traditionally kebabs are cooked over charcoal, which gives them an inimitable flavour. The favourite meat is lamb, but occasionally beef is used instead.

If Turkey has the rich traditions of the Ottoman Empire to sustain it, then Greece, by contrast, has a more frugal, peasant tradition. The food is vibrant, colourful and fresh – less heavily spiced than Turkish food but with an abundant use of aromatic herbs such as thyme, rosemary, fennel and oregano. Lemon juice adds zest to simple dishes, and the famous egg and lemon sauce, *avgolemono* is served with fish, meat and chicken, the lemon cutting the richness of the eggs. Olive oil is the cooking medium of choice, and olives are as much a symbol of Greek cuisine as they are of Italian. Fish is abundant – octopus, tuna, squid, red mullet, shellfish – and so fresh that it needs little more than grilling with herbs, olive oil and lemon juice. Greece shares with Turkey a passion for vegetable dishes, and in particular for aubergines and courgettes, which are served in countless inventive ways. White beans are a speciality: used to make *fassolada*, a thick soup that is virtually the Greek national dish, and a variety of casseroles and salads.

Like much of the Balkan area, Greece enjoys sticky, syrup-drenched pastries, such as the nut-filled *baklava*, and *loukoumades*, little cinnamon-scented fritters. Yet one of the glories of Greek life is its wonderful array of fresh fruit: apples, figs, oranges, grapes, melons. Accompanied by a bowl of thick sheep's milk yogurt and a drizzle of honey, there can hardly be a better way to end a meal.

It is often mistakenly assumed that Cypriot cooking differs little from that of Greece. In fact, although there are many similarities, Cyprus also has much in common with its Arab neighbours, including a fondness for bulghur wheat and pulses, such as lentils, split peas and chickpeas, and the use of masses of coriander. Vegetable dishes are many and varied, while salads are often made with simply dressed, lightly boiled greens. Baking is a strong point: rich, flaky savoury pies; *elioti*, a bread enriched with olive oil and dotted with olives; and sweet pastries such as *loukoumades*.

Although the cooking of Turkey, Greece and Cyprus is familiar to many who have taken holidays in these countries, Albania is rather more of a mystery. This small, mountainous country was long part of the Ottoman Empire, and many of its dishes show a Turkish ancestry, including *dolma*, *köfte*, *baklava* and stuffed vegetables. A selection of *meze* dishes is still a popular way to eat. An Italian influence, however, means that pasta is immensely popular, and there is a variety of different shapes. Other staples include bread, cheese and yogurt, or *kos*, which is made mainly from cows' milk but also from sheep's, goats' and buffaloes' milk.

sieving and straining

The reasons for sieving and straining ingredients are as varied as the dishes themselves. The basic action of sieving is to incorporate air as well as break down the size of the lumps or particles. The texture of the food can also be refined by passing it through a fine sieve. The action of straining is simply to separate liquids from the solids. This may be in order to keep the solids and discard the liquid or visa versa, or to use the two in different ways in the same recipe.

1 Food mill This will mash or purée food as well as remove any unwanted seeds or pips etc. They come with a selection of discs with different size holes (producing coarser or smoother results) through which the food is pushed as the handle is turned.

2 Sourotouris This is similar to a standard colander with a raised base enabling it to stand by itself. When cooking a large quantity of food this is much easier to use than a handled sieve. The food can drain for any length of time, such as the salted cucumber in *cacik*.

3 Cheesecloth Originally used only in cheese production, this cloth has a multitude of uses. Its fine light mesh is perfect for filtering out the tiniest of particles in stocks and sauces. You can also remove the last traces of liquid from cooked spinach by wrapping it in the cheesecloth and then squeezing out every last drop.

4 Strainer (chinois) The conical shape of the strainer allows the liquid to flow down the outside towards the tip and into a smaller size bowl or pan. The fine mesh produces a very smooth result. These are often used with a type of wooden pusher that forces the solids through the mesh along with the liquid.

5 Modern koskino This is a large shallow sieve used for sifting flour especially in bread making. Its wide area makes it perfect for covering a large worktop space as well as incorporating as much air as possible into the flour.

6 Old-style koskino Similar to the modern *koskino*, this drum sieve is slightly larger and shallower. The drum is made from the wood while the mesh would originally have been made from silk. Today they are often made from nylon but still produce the same perfect results.

mussels stuffed with rice

midia pilafi

Greek flavours are often very subtle, never overpowering. This mussel dish is one I enjoyed in a *taverna* on the Greek island of Crete many years ago – a great way to enjoy the delicate molluscs. On festive occasions this pilaf is sometimes served cold, but does not compare to the hot dish.

Serves 4
Preparation Time: 50 minutes

Ingredients

1.5kg fresh live mussels
25g unsalted butter
1 tbsp virgin olive oil
1 onion, finely chopped
200g long grain rice
freshly ground black
    pepper
2 tbsp chopped dill
3 spring onions, finely
    chopped
lemon wedges, to
    garnish

Tools

2 large pans or
    casseroles
Colander
Wooden spoon

Method

1 Scrub the mussels with a stiff brush under cold running water. Debeard them and place in a large pan, discarding any mussels that may be open. Pour 200ml water over and bring to the boil over a high heat until they open. Strain in a colander, reserving the cooking liquid.

2 Heat the butter and oil in a large pan or casserole, add the onion and cook for 1–2 minutes until softened. Stir in the rice and coat with the butter, stirring with a wooden spoon.

3 Measure the reserved cooking liquid, then add enough water to make 375ml in total. Pour over the rice, add a little pepper, the dill and return to the boil; cover and simmer the rice for 20 minutes or until tender, remove and cover with a teacloth, replace the lid, and let stand for 10 minutes.

4 Remove the cooked mussels from the shells, roughly chop them, and add to the rice along with the spring onions and mix well.

5 Take about 48 of the mussel shells, then fill them generously with the pilaff, making sure you have mussel pieces in each shell. Arrange on a large dish, garnish with lemon and serve.

greek fig rolls
fig kadaifi

Kadaifi (or *kataifi*) is shredded dough which is used to wrap a sweet filling, traditionally made from ground walnuts, pistachios and sometimes soft cheese, and coated in a cinnamon flavoured syrup. One day I experimented filling the strands with a dried fig and nut filling, which to me tasted as good if not better than the original.

Serves 4 (makes 15 rolls)
Preparation Time: 1 hour 15 minutes plus chilling overnight

Tools
Blender
Bowl
Wooden spoon
Brush
Baking sheet
Saucepan
Sharp knife

Ingredients
300g *kadaifi* pastry
50g unsalted butter,
   melted
2 tbsp icing sugar

For the filling
150g dried figs
50g raisins
100ml Greek honey
1 tsp grated lemon zest
1 tsp ground cinnamon
pinch of ground nutmeg
pinch of ground cloves
75g whole blanched
   almonds, toasted,
   coarsely chopped
50g walnuts, toasted,
   coarsely chopped

For the syrup
125g caster sugar
1 tbsp lemon juice
5cm piece cinnamon stick
1 tbsp Greek honey

Method
1 Preheat the oven to 180°C/Gas 4. Make the filling: place the figs and raisins in a blender and whiz to a coarse purée. Place in a bowl, add the remaining ingredients, mix together, chill overnight.
2 Carefully unwrap the *kadaifi* pastry and spread out on a flat surface. Take one third of the pastry with strands running lengthways, cut to a 15 x 20cm rectangle. Brush the strands all over with some of the melted butter, then dust liberally with icing sugar.
3 Spread one third of the filling at the end of the pastry, then roll up firmly into a neat roll. Repeat with the remaining pastry and filling.
4 Place the three prepared rolls on a baking sheet, close together, and bake for 30 minutes until golden.
5 Meanwhile, make the syrup. Dissolve the sugar and 75ml water in a pan over a low heat and add the lemon juice. Bring to the boil, add the cinnamon and simmer for 10 minutes. Stir in the honey, strain and keep warm.
6 Remove the rolls from the oven, pour the warm syrup over and leave to cool. Using a sharp knife, cut each roll into 5 pieces and serve at room temperature.

pans

While some professional chefs may say that every pan is its own particular use, other home cooks will make their one favourite pan do everything all of the time. It is however true that some pans of differing sizes and substances are best suited to their own style of cooking. For example a heavy cast iron pan will slowly come to the correct temperature but once there will cook extremely evenly and consistently while a light aluminium pan will be far more responsive to differing temperatures and so will stop cooking the food as soon as it is removed from the heat. Choose the correct pan and the results will be perfect.

1 Kazan A large heavy based pan like this is ideal for all sorts of recipes that require a long slow cooking process like the squash and aubergine pilaf. A tight fitting lid is essential so the food inside does not dry out.

2 Tava This Turkish frying pan with a long handle was originally made from cast iron, so conducts the heat very evenly. It is ideal for sautéing vegetables or small amounts of fish or meat and only requires a little oil. You can also use these pans for dry-frying spices and seeds to give them a toasted flavour.

3 Saganaki The popular Greek appetiser of the same name was traditionally made in this pan and hence gave it its name. While it is not a wide shallow frying pan like the ones we use today, this deep lidded pan is just the right pan for this Greek dish. Made of hard-wearing aluminium it will last for many years.

4 Tencere The heat-toughened glass lid to this pan is very useful when cooking food that needs a watchful eye. Enamelled on the outside and non-stick on the inside this makes it easier to cook with very little fat. The two handles allow this pan to be easily carried to the table when feeding a crowd.

fried cheese with tomato, olive and bean salad

haloumi saganaki

Haloumi cheese is one of the favourite cheeses of Cyprus, Greece and the Lebanon, and is made in many family homes from sheep's, goats' or cows' milk. It is a somewhat rubbery cheese, and it needs either frying or grilling extremely quickly – when it browns it is transformed into something special. A *saganaki* is the small double-handled pan in which typical *meze* are prepared in Cyprus and Greece and brought directly to the table.

Serves 4
Preparation Time: 35 minutes

Ingredients

1 block haloumi cheese, soaked in hot water for 5 minutes, dried
½ tsp sweet paprika
4 tbsp virgin olive oil
juice of ½ lemon

12 black olives, pitted
1 tbsp superfine capers, rinsed and drained
1 small red onion, finely chopped
salt and freshly ground black pepper

For the salad

1 garlic clove, peeled
juice of ¼ lemon
4 tbsp olive oil
2 tbsp fresh coriander
1 tbsp chopped fresh mint
120g cooked white haricots beans
12 yellow cherry tomatoes, quartered

Tools

Knife
Cutting board
Salad bowl
Frying pan or *saganaki*

Method

1 For the salad, with a knife, smash the garlic clove flat on a chopping board, then rub it over the inside of the bowl. Add the lemon juice, olive oil and herbs and mix well. Add the remaining ingredients, season to taste, leave to marinate for 20 minutes at room temperature.

2 Cut the haloumi into 4 x 1cm thick slices, dip them into cold water, and dust with paprika.

3 Heat a frying pan or *saganaki* with the oil and when hot add the haloumi and fry until golden for 1 minute each side. Drizzle the lemon juice over.

4 Arrange the salad on individual serving plates, top each with an slice of fried cheese, spoon the lemon- and oil-flavoured pan juices over and serve immediately.

cold fish in tomato and olive oil sauce
balik pilakisi

Cold fish dishes are not extremely popular in Britain, whereas in the Middle Eastern countries they are revered. Until I tried this recipe, I have to say I had reservations about it, but I am now fully converted. Use a good quality oil in the making of the sauce: it will pay dividends.

Serves 4
Preparation Time: 1 hour 10 minutes including 30 minutes chilling

Method

1 Heat a large frying pan with 3 tbsp of the oil. Score the fish down to the bone with 3 slashes on each side. Season all over, then add to the hot oil and cook for 2–3 minutes on each side until golden; remove from the pan and set aside.

2 Return the pan to the heat, add the garlic, onions and carrot and cook over a low heat until they soften. Add the tomatoes, tomato purée and 200ml water. Bring to the boil and simmer for 15 minutes.

3 Return the fish to the sauce, then spoon some of the sauce over the fish.

4 Pour the remaining olive oil over, simmer on a low heat for 15 minutes, or until the fish are tender. Remove from the heat and cool until cold.

5 With a fish slice, place the fish on a serving dish, coat with the sauce. Squeeze the juice of the lemon over, and serve garnished with lemon wedges.

Ingredients

125ml virgin olive oil
1kg red mullet or snapper, left whole, cleaned
salt and freshly ground black pepper
4 garlic cloves, crushed
2 onions, thinly sliced
1 carrot, thinly sliced
400g canned tomatoes, chopped
2 tsp tomato purée
½ lemon
lemon wedges, to garnish

Tools

Large frying pan
Sharp knife
Fish slice
Spoon

serving dishes

Many Balkan dishes are cooked over direct heat and then transferred to earthenware serving dishes. Because the food comes to the table – along with its aromas – the appearance of the dish is also very important. Most of these are earthenware and some are fired at a high enough temperature to make them oven-proof. The dishes illustrated here are the traditional ones of the Balkans but any similar ones can be used at home.

1, 2 Tava These are both Greek dishes – although they have the same name as the Turkish frying pan. Some have a shiny glaze while others are unglazed, but they all have a well-fitting lid. This enables the food within to stay hot for longer. This also means that the food is easily transportable for the many communal meals that Greek families enjoy.

3 Tepsi This is a large shallow glazed dish, which sometimes will have handles. Originating from Turkey this dish is ideal for hot layered dishes such as Chicken Mousaka or for cool salads.

4 Guivec These are Turkish oval dishes of varying sizes depending on how much food is to be served. They are very attractive dishes to cook in as well as bring to the table for stews such as Saksuka.

5 Small round *meze* dishes Different forms of *meze* appear all through the Balkans and these small earthenware dishes will hold just about any of them. A large table can be dotted with many of these holding anything from spiced olives to stuffed vine leaves.

vegetarian *meze*
small vegetarian platters

A large feature of Mediterranean hospitality is the serving of small dishes at the table, called *meze* in the Balkans, *mezze* in Lebanon and Syria. The different varieties of *meze* will always be served with local breads. Here is a small selection of Turkish-style *meze*, to give you a flavour of the country, traditionally served in small dishes on a large circular tray called a *tepsi*.

All Serve 4–6

bulghur salad (*kisir*)

Ingredients
50g dried pomegranate seeds
150g bulghur wheat
2 tomatoes, skinned, seeded, finely chopped
1 onion, finely chopped
¼ each green and red pepper, seeded, finely chopped
120g chopped fresh flat-leaf parsley
75g chopped fresh mint
4 tbsp virgin olive oil
1 tsp pomegranate molasses or lemon juice
¼ tsp hot paprika
salt and freshly ground black pepper

Method
1 Soak the pomegranate seeds for 30 minutes, and then drain thoroughly.
2 Place the bulghur wheat in a bowl, gradually stir in 150ml boiling water, a little at a time, cover and leave for 15 minutes at room temperature.
3 Add all remaining ingredients and season to taste. Fluff the salad up with a fork and serve.

aubergine caviar

Ingredients
1 aubergine
100ml virgin olive oil
1 red pepper, seeded, cut into small dice
2 garlic cloves, crushed
½ tsp ground cumin
¼ tsp hot paprika
2 tbsp chopped fresh flat-leaf parsley

Method
1 Preheat oven to 200°C/Gas 6. Cut the aubergine in half lengthways, place in a baking tin and pour over 60ml of the olive oil. Roast in the oven for 25–30 minutes, remove and let cool.
2 In a frying pan, heat the remaining oil, add the diced pepper, garlic, cumin and paprika and cook over a low heat for 5–6 minutes until the peppers are soft.
3 Spoon out the inner flesh from the aubergine on to a cutting board, then chop firmly; add to the pan with the parsley, cook for 5 minutes and season to taste. Serve hot or cold.

beetroot salad (*pancar salatasi*)

Ingredients
150g raw beetroots, washed
1 tbsp white wine vinegar
2 tbsp olive or sunflower oil
½ tsp ground cumin
1 small red onion, thinly sliced
8 black olives, pitted
4 red radishes, thinly sliced
100g feta cheese, crumbled
pinch of sweet paprika

Method
1 Cook the beetroots in boiling salted water until tender. Drain, reserving 3 tbsp of the cooking liquid. Allow to cool, peel and cut into small wedges.
2 Place the beetroots in a bowl, add the reserved cooking liquid and the remaining ingredients except feta and paprika. Mix well and marinate for 30 minutes.
3 Sprinkle the feta cheese and paprika over and serve.

cucumber yogurt relish (*cacik*)

Ingredients
½ medium cucumber, cut into slices or diced
salt and freshly ground black pepper
100ml natural Greek yogurt
40g raisins, soaked in warm water until plump, dried
2 tbsp virgin olive oil
25g chopped walnuts
2 tbsp chopped fresh dill
1 garlic clove, crushed

Method
1 Place the cucumber in a colander, sprinkle liberally with salt and leave to drain for 30 minutes. Rinse the cucumber and pat dry.
2 Transfer the cucumber to a bowl, add the yogurt, and mix well. Add the remaining ingredients, season to taste and serve.

grilling

Cooking over hot coals is one of the oldest forms of cooking and still gives food a wonderful flavour. You do not need to use a large built-in barbecue, there are now small and even disposable barbecue grills which will give a great result. A few key tools are necessary such as long-handled tongs and forks to protect your hands and get the best from grilling.

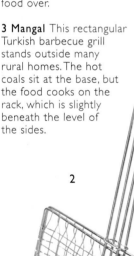

1 Foufou This is a large Greek barbecue grill standing on four legs. The round drum shape enables the heat to spread evenly around the total surface area. The hot coals sit in the base of the drum, then the food is placed on a grill rack resting on the metal protruding shapes above.

2 Grilling rack A large double rack that is hinged together at one side with long handles on the opposite side. The food is sandwiched between the two racks and then placed over the coals. This makes it much easier to turn the food over.

3 Mangal This rectangular Turkish barbecue grill stands outside many rural homes. The hot coals sit at the base, but the food cooks on the rack, which is slightly beneath the level of the sides.

4 Metal skewers A huge variety of foods can be threaded on these long metal rods and grilled quickly over the hot coals in any barbecue. They are known as *sis* in Turkey and *souvles* in Greece.

5 Wooden skewers Some foods to be brought to the table on skewers are more suited to these long wooden skewers. Since the wood can easily burn over the hot coals, it is important to soak them in water first for at least 30 minutes.

grilled fish over embers with sumac
balik izgarasi

In Turkey, fish and seafood dishes play a major role in the country's eating habits, understandably perhaps as it is surrounded by sea. Turkey's best seafood dishes come from the Black Sea coast. All manner of fish are prepared grilled, baked, stuffed in homes and in restaurants. This simple grilled fish recipe cooked on *sis* (metal skewers) is seasoned with sumac, a sour red berry grown all over the Middle East mild, yet with a distinctively sour fruity taste which is an important ingredient in dishes like *fatoosh* (bread salad) and some *kibbe* and vegetable dishes. The ideal accompaniment for this recipe is a classic Turkish *pilavi* made with broad beans and dill.

Serves 4 (makes 8 sis kebabs)
Preparation Time: 3 hours 20 minutes including marinating

Tools	Ingredients	Method
Sharp knife	400g tuna fillet, skinless	**1** Cut the fish into large bite size chunks, place in a shallow dish.
Cutting board	400g swordfish fillet, skinless	**2** Make the marinade: mix the onion juice, half the lemon juice, 4 tbsp of the oil, the sumac, bay leaves and seasoning. Stir the mixture, pour over the fish pieces, cover with clingfilm, and place in the refrigerator for 2–3 hours.
Shallow dish	lemon slices, to garnish	
Large bowl	flat-leaf parsley, to garnish	
Small bowl		
8 metal skewers (*sis*)	**For the marinade**	**3** Before cooking, in a small bowl, mix the remaining oil and lemon juice to baste the fish while cooking. Thread the fish chunks on to 8 metal skewers (*sis*), ensuring that each has a selection of each fish.
Charcoal grill or pan grill	2 onions, grated, strained to give juice only	
	juice of 1 lemon	
	6 tbsp virgin olive oil	**4** Place the skewers on a preheated charcoal grill or pan grill to cook, brushing them regularly with the lemon baste, for 4–5 minutes until cooked and slightly charred.
	1 tbsp sumac	
	3 bay leaves, shredded	
	salt and freshly ground black pepper	**5** Serve the fish kebabs on a bed of the *pilavi*, garnish with lemon slices and parsley.

Note
A *tarator* sauce would be an excellent sauce to serve with these kebabs (see page 102). I also like to serve a simple yogurt sauce with them.

Pilavi

Tools	Ingredients	Method
Large pan with a lid	200g long grain rice	**1** Prior to cooking, soak the rice well in hot water for 15 minutes until the water runs clear.
Wooden spoon	25g unsalted butter or 2 tbsp olive oil	**2** Heat the butter or oil in a pan, add the onion, cover and cook over a low heat until they are softened. Add the dill, cook for 30 seconds; add the rice, stir well with a wooden spoon and season with a little salt and pepper.
Teacloth	1 onion, finely chopped	
	2 tbsp chopped fresh dill	
	salt and freshly ground black pepper	
	500ml chicken stock or water	**3** Pour the stock over, bring to the boil without stirring; reduce the heat, cover, and simmer gently for 20 minutes.
	350g shelled broad beans	**4** Remove from the heat, add the broad beans and then place a teacloth over the rice to cover. Replace the lid, leave the *pilavi* to stand for 10 minutes. Fluff up the rice to incorporate the beans and serve.

chargrilled meatballs with feta
keftedakia

Keftedes are small Greek rissoles made of finely ground meat, which can also be known as 'bifteki'. They can be fried in olive oil or chargrilled, and stuffed with cheese as in this recipe. They make a great cocktail food, in Greece they are usually served as part of a *meze* selection. The meatballs may be filled with other cheeses, such as Greek *kefalotiri*. Serve them with a Greek-style salad.

Serves 4
Preparation Time: 1 hour 30 minutes

Method

1 Place the bread in a bowl, add 100ml of water, soak for 10 minutes, then remove and squeeze out the excess water with your hands.
2 In another large bowl, place the minced lamb with the bread, add the onion, lemon juice and herbs, mix well.
3 Beat the egg well and add to the minced lamb, mixing thoroughly; season to taste. Cover with clingfilm and place in the refrigerator for 1 hour.
4 Wet your hands then shape the lamb mixture into small balls approximately 4cm in diameter. Make a small indentation in each meatball and insert a piece of feta cheese. Close up the filling and reform into balls, ensuring that the cheese is enclosed within, return to the refrigerator until needed.
5 Heat a charcoal grill (*foufou*) or pan grill. Thread the meat balls on to small wooden (pre-soaked) skewers. Brush the meatballs all over with the oil, then grill for 4–5 minutes until golden and browned all over.
6 Garnish with lemon wedges and serve with a Greek-style salad.

Note

Feta can be a little salty, I recommend soaking it in warm water for 10 minutes, then drain and dry it.

Ingredients

3 slices stale white bread
750g finely minced lamb
1 onion, grated
juice of 1 lemon
1 tbsp chopped fresh
   flat-leaf parsley
1 tbsp chopped fresh
   oregano
1 egg
salt and freshly ground
   black pepper
125g feta cheese, in 1cm
   cubes (see Note)
vegetable oil for grilling
1 lemon, cut into
   wedges, to garnish

Tools

2 large bowls
Wooden spoon
Whisk
Clingfilm
Charcoal grill
Wooden skewers
   (pre-soaked in water)
Brush

stuffed lamb chops on aubergine skordalia

Prepare the recipe in the summer, when the barbecue beckons. The flavours are wonderful, the *skordalia* delicious and creamy, serve with lots of bread and a large bowl of salad. *Skordalia* (or *skorthalia*) is usually made with potatoes — the aubergine makes a great variation.

Serves 4
Preparation Time: 1 hour 15 minutes

Ingredients

2 tbsp virgin olive oil
   plus extra for brushing
   and drizzling
120g fresh spinach,
   stems removed
1 onion, finely chopped
½ tsp ground cinnamon
salt and freshly ground
   black pepper
100g finely minced lamb
1 egg yolk
4 x double rib lamb
   chops, 5cm thick,
   slightly flattened
1 tsp ground cumin
1 tsp fresh oregano
   leaves
lemon wedges, to
   garnish
fresh thyme leaves,
   to garnish

For the *skordalia*

1 large aubergine
2 garlic cloves, peeled
6 tbsp virgin olive oil
75g ground almonds
75g fresh white
   breadcrumbs
120ml full fat milk or
   single cream

Tools

Frying pan
Colander
Small sharp knife
Bowl
Spoon
Toothpicks
Brush
Baking sheet
Blender
Barbecue rack
   or pan grill

Method

1 Preheat the oven to 200°C/Gas 6. To prepare the stuffing, heat a frying pan with half the oil, add the spinach, cook over a high heat for 1 minute, then drain in a colander. Squeeze out any excess moisture by hand, then finely chop.
2 Return the frying pan to the heat, add the remaining oil, and when hot, add the onion and cinnamon; cook for 2–3 minutes until the onion is soft and tender. Add the chopped spinach, cook for 2 minutes and season to taste. Transfer to a bowl and allow to cool.
3 Add the minced lamb to the cold spinach mix, then add the egg yolk and adjust the seasoning.
4 Using a sharp knife, cut a deep pocket into the side of each lamb chop, ensuring that you don't cut it right through. Open each pocket gently with your fingers, then fill each with a good amount of the lamb stuffing, and secure with toothpicks. Brush the chops all over with olive oil, season well with cumin, salt and pepper, and sprinkle the oregano over. Place in the refrigerator until needed.
5 For the *skordalia*, with a sharp knife, pierce holes all over the aubergine, place the aubergine and garlic cloves on a large sheet of foil, drizzle over 2 tbsp of the oil, then scrunch up the foil, to form a pouch. Place on a baking sheet, bake for 25–30 minutes, then remove from foil and cool. When cold, cut the aubergine in half, then scoop out the inner pulp flesh with a spoon.
6 Place the aubergine flesh and cooked garlic in a blender, add the almonds, breadcrumbs and milk, and whiz to a smooth purée. Finally, drizzle in the oil with the motor running, season to taste, and keep warm.
7 Place the lamb chops on a barbecue rack and chargrill (ideally over charcoal) or pan grill until cooked, about 3–4 minutes each side.
8 Serve the chop on the *skordalia*, drizzled with a little olive oil and garnished with lemon wedges and fresh thyme leaves.

wrapped pittas with grilled vegetables
vegetable souvlakia

The name *souvlakia* comes from the name of the metal skewers (*souvles*) often used in this dish. Here we use wooden ones. They are more often threaded with cubes of lamb, marinated and chargrilled to make *arni souvlaki*. They are then wrapped in warm pitta bread and drizzled with yogurt.

Serves 4
Preparation Time: 1 hour 20 minutes including marinating

Ingredients
4 tbsp olive oil
juice of 1 lemon
1 tsp dried thyme
1 tsp dried oregano
1 garlic clove, crushed
1 bay leaf
salt and freshly ground
    black pepper
1 green pepper, seeded,
    cut into 5cm cubes
1 large courgette,
    cut into 2.5cm thick
    rounds
4 firm tomatoes, halved,
    seeded
1 long thin aubergine,
    cut into 2.5cm thick
    rounds
1 red onion, cut into
    small wedges
8 large button
    mushrooms
4 warm freshly baked
    pitta breads, to serve

For the yogurt sauce
100ml natural Greek
    yogurt
1 tbsp chopped fresh
    mint
1 garlic clove, crushed
¼ tsp ground cumin

Tools
2 bowls
Charcoal grill or pan
    grill
4 wooden skewers
    (pre-soaked in water)
    or metal skewers
    (*souvles*)
Brush

Method
1 In a bowl, mix the oil, lemon juice and dried herbs. Add the garlic, bay leaf, and a little salt and pepper.
2 Add the vegetables, toss well together, leave to marinate for 45 minutes–1 hour at room temperature.
3 Preheat the barbecue grill or pan grill. Thread the vegetables in alternating order and with an eye to colour on to 4 large wooden or metal skewers.
4 Brush the vegetables with some of the marinade all over, then place on the grill, turning them regularly, while continuing basting with the marinade until charred and cooked, about 20 minutes.
5 Meanwhile, make the sauce by combining all the ingredients in a bowl.
6 Remove the vegetables from the grill, lay a skewer on top of each pitta and carefully pull out the skewer, top with a good spoonful of yogurt sauce, then roll up the bread to form a wrap around the meat, serve immediately and enjoy!

baking

Cooking food in the oven in an uncovered dish will produce very different results. There is a wide surface area which means that more of the liquid is able to evaporate. This in turn means that the flavours are intensified and the food is allowed to brown on top. Choose the appropriate size dish for the food you are cooking from small individual serving size to large platter size.

1 Turkish tepsi Made out of one sheet of metal these traditional dishes are relatively flat with gently sloping sides. They are commonly used for baking the Turkish flatbread called *pide*.

2, 3 Tepsi Made of lightweight metal and with straight sides, these dishes heat up quickly and so will cook food in a shorter time. They are well suited to deep dense dishes such as Mousaka and rich cakes.

4 Greek baking dishes Available in several sizes these glazed baking dishes have a handle making serving easier. They are totally ovenproof as well as being attractive enough to bring to the table. The smaller ones can be used for cooking any small portions of food, but are commonly used for vegetables and eggs.

turkish pizza

Flatbreads have been an important element of the Middle Eastern countries for centuries, each has their own beloved types which they consider better than their neighbours. The Turkish *pide* is the most famous flatbread. It makes an excellent pizza dough base that can be topped with any amount of unusual toppings – this one is filled with minced lamb topped with *sudschuk* or spicy sausage, and cooked with eggs. *Pide* is especially important as a quick snack eaten in the evening during the fast of Ramadan.

Serves 8
Preparation Time: 50 minutes

Ingredients

For the dough

30g fresh yeast or
   7g sachet fast acting
   yeast
pinch of sugar
250ml warm water
500g plain flour
1 tsp salt
1 tbsp virgin olive oil,
   plus extra for brushing
1 egg yolk

For the topping

400g finely minced lamb
4 tomatoes, skinned,
   seeded, chopped
1 onion, finely chopped
3 tbsp chopped fresh
   flat-leaf parsley
2 garlic cloves
½ tbsp tomato purée
½ tsp dried red chilli
   flakes
pinch of sugar
salt and freshly ground
   black pepper
200g sliced Turkish
   sausage (sudschuk)
2 eggs, lightly beaten

Method

1 Dissolve the yeast and sugar in half the water. Sift the flour into a bowl, add the salt, pour in the dissolved yeast and stir well. Add the remaining water to bring it to a dough. Knead until smooth and pliable, 8–10 minutes. Return the dough to a clean bowl, cover with a warm damp teacloth, leave in a warm place for 1 hour or until dough has risen and doubled in volume.

2 Preheat oven to 220°C/Gas 7. Knead the dough again for 5 minutes, then roll out on a floured work surface to a rectangle big enough to fit a large baking tray (about 20 x 30cm).

3 Brush the baking tray lightly with some oil then place the dough on it. Mix the egg yolk and oil, and use this to brush the dough all over. Set aside.

4 For the topping, place all the ingredients together in a bowl except for the sausage and eggs, seasoning to taste.

5 Spread the mix over the dough, then bring the edges of the dough up slightly to form a crust. Top with the sausage.

6 Place in the oven to bake for 15–20 minutes, then remove and drizzle the beaten egg over the surface, return to the oven and cook for 5 minutes until the egg is just set. Remove and cool before cutting into portions.

Tools

1 small bowl
2 large bowls
Rolling pin
Large baking tray
Brush
Palette knife
Sharp knife

Note

In Turkey, an onion relish called *sogam piyazi* is traditionally served with this dish and kebabs. Simply slice some onions, mix with chopped fresh flat-leaf parsley and a little sumac, and serve with the pizza: delicious.

Ingredients

4 tbsp virgin olive oil
25g unsalted butter
2 aubergines, cut into
  large cubes
1 small butternut squash,
  cut into large cubes
1 onion, sliced
50g currants
30g pine nuts
1 tsp ground cinnamon
200g long grain rice,
  soaked in hot water
  for 15 minutes and
  drained well
100g vermicelli noodles,
  broken into 2.5cm pieces
1 tbsp tomato purée
1 tsp caster sugar
1 tbsp chopped fresh
  flat-leaf parsley
1 tbsp chopped fresh mint
500ml vegetable stock
  or water
6 sheets Turkish *yufka*
  or filo pastry
50g unsalted butter, melted

Tools

Heavy based pan
Wooden spoon
Brush
20cm springform tin

Method

1 Preheat oven to 190°C/Gas 5. Heat the oil and butter in heavy based pan. Add the vegetables and fry until lightly golden for 8–10 minutes. Add the currants, pine nuts and cinnamon and cook for a further 2 minutes.

2 Add the rice and vermicelli, and stir into the vegetables. Stir in the tomato purée, sugar and herbs, then pour on the stock. Bring to the boil, cover with a lid, reduce the heat and simmer for 30 minutes.

3 Remove from the heat, remove the lid, cover with a teacloth, then replace the lid and leave to stand for 10 minutes.

4 Brush one of the pastry sheets with melted butter, top with second sheet, brush again, then top with a third sheet, and brush with butter. Prepare the other 3 sheets the same way.

5 Cut the prepared sheets into 9cm-wide strips, then line a greased 20cm springform tin with the strips (1), slightly overlapping each other and leaving enough pastry overhanging the edge of the dish to enclose the filling.

6 Fill the pastry with the pilaf, then fold the overhanging pastry to the centre to enclose the filling (2). Brush the top with a little more butter. Place on a baking sheet.

7 Place in the oven and bake for 20 minutes. Invert on to a serving dish and cut into wedges to reveal the filling. Serve with dill-flavoured yogurt sauce.

Note

To make a dill-yogurt sauce, simply combine 120g yogurt with 3 tablespoons chopped fresh dill and season to taste with salt and freshly ground black pepper. Mix thoroughly and serve.

1

2

squash and aubergine pilaf in a pastry jacket
yufkali pilavi

Yufka is the Turkish equivalent of Greek filo pastry – very thin sheets. Once extensively made in homes nowadays it can be purchased in Turkish shops made by *yufkaci* (*yufka* bakers). Filo makes an excellent substitute as does spring roll pastry. This dish of vegetable pilaf in pastry makes an impressive vegetarian dish – serve it with a dill and yogurt sauce and a cucumber salad.

Serves 4–6
Preparation Time: 1 hour 15 minutes

casseroles

The casserole is the perfect make-ahead meal. These stews are often made with tougher vegetables or cuts of meat that require longer cooking and actually improve on being allowed to stand and then reheated the following day. They are sometimes covered with a lid or can easily be covered with foil. These are all safe in the oven but not flame-proof so should not be placed over direct heat.

1 **Tava** Similar to the serving dish of the same name, this ovenproof one is used as a casserole. The domed lid allows the steam to collect and fall back into the stew, not loosing any of the precious cooking liquid.

2 **Tsoukali** This is the mainstay of most Greek kitchens. The heavy earthenware casserole has bowed sides increasing the capacity while the tops narrows slightly to let less of the moisture escape.

3 **Giouvetsi** A wide and shallow casserole, perfect for cooking lighter foods such as fish or chicken. The dish can be covered with foil or the food topped with sliced potatoes to keep the juices in.

4 **Small round baking dish** You can cook vegetable or grain accompaniments in these smaller dishes. They are also useful for keeping leftovers and then reheating.

oven baked vegetable stew
saksuka

The making of *saksuka* dates back to the Ottoman period. It was cooked in a casserole-style dish called a *guivec* which was the name given to all casseroles whether made of vegetables or meat. Connoisseurs say that this was the forerunner of the Mediterranean ratatouille, the much loved vegetable dish of France.

Serves 4–6
Preparation Time: 1 hour 10 minutes

Ingredients

300g small potatoes,
  peeled
2 long thin aubergines
2 red peppers, seeded
2 green peppers, seeded
1 onion, peeled
2 garlic cloves, crushed
salt and freshly ground
  black pepper
1 tsp sweet paprika
2 tbsp chopped fresh dill
1 tbsp chopped fresh
  mint
1 tbsp chopped fresh
  flat-leaf parsley
100ml virgin olive oil
juice of ½ lemon
6 medium tomatoes,
  halved
1 tsp caster sugar

Method

1 Preheat the oven to 190°C/Gas 5. Cut the potatoes and aubergines into 2.5cm thick slices, and cut the peppers and onion into large cubes. Place all the vegetables except the tomatoes in a large ovenproof casserole, add the garlic. Season liberally with salt, pepper and little paprika. Scatter the herbs over. Mix half the oil with 300ml of water and the lemon juice, mix thoroughly, and add to the casserole.

2 Lay the tomatoes over the top, sprinkle a little sugar on top and pour the remaining oil over.

3 Place in the oven for 25 minutes, then reduce the heat to 150°C/Gas 2 for a further 45 minutes or until the vegetables are tender and tomatoes golden.

4 Serve hot from the oven with lots of bread to mop up the casserole juices. It is also delicious served cold.

Tools

Sharp knife
Chopping board
Ovenproof casserole

Ingredients

4 tbsp virgin olive oil

8 boneless quails, cut into small dice

salt and freshly ground black pepper

1 onion, finely chopped

4 tomatoes, skinned, seeded, chopped

60g raisins

½ tsp ground cumin

¼ tsp ground cinnamon

2 tbsp chopped fresh coriander

1 tbsp chopped fresh mint

650ml chicken stock

125g *pourgouri* (bulghur wheat)

20 fresh vine leaves, blanched in boiling water then refreshed in cold water

50g ready to eat dried apricots

juice of ½ lemon

25g unsalted butter

coriander flowers, to garnish *(optional)*

Method

1 Heat the oil in a large frying pan; when hot, add the diced seasoned quails and fry 2–3 minutes until sealed and golden. Add the onion, tomatoes and half the raisins, and cook for a further 5 minutes. Season with cumin, cinnamon, coriander and mint; mix well.

2 Pour 150ml of the stock over and bring to the boil; add the bulghur wheat, cover with a lid, and reduce the heat. Simmer for 15 minutes until the wheat is cooked and all liquid absorbed. Remove the *pilafi* to a tray, leave to go cold. Preheat oven to 200°C/Gas 6.

3 Lay out the vine leaves on a flat surface, shiny side down. Place a spoonful of the quail *pilafi* on each leaf near the stem end, then fold in the end and sides and roll up neatly. Repeat until all the leaves are filled.

4 Place the wrapped vine leaves in a large ovenproof casserole with a lid, laying flat. Scatter the apricots and remaining raisins over, then cover with the remaining stock, lemon juice and small pieces of butter. Cover with the lid and cook in the oven or on the stove for 35–40 minutes.

5 Transfer to a serving dish and pour over the pan juices. Garnish with coriander flowers if you like.

Tools

Large frying pan with lid
Wooden spoon
Ovenproof casserole

vine leaves stuffed
with quail and pourgouri pilafi

In this delicately flavoured dish from Greece, diced young quails are cooked with *pourgouri* (bulghur wheat), a staple in the Balkan and Arabic world, then wrapped in vine leaves. The hulled wheat has a nutty flavour very popular with vegetarians and those following a natural food diet. It is available in fine and coarse varieties from Middle Eastern stores and health food shops.

Serves 4
Preparation Time: 1 hour 20 minutes

stifado

Stifado, or *stifatho*, is the renowned Greek beef stew made with copious amounts of onions, cooked with red wine and spiced with sweet cinnamon. In Greece it can be made with octopus and other seafood, cooked traditionally in an earthenware casserole. This wonderful recipe is with the kind permission of one of Britain's best loved food writers, sophie grigson.

Serves 6–8
Preparation Time: 2 hours 50 minutes

Method

1 Cut the meat into large chunks of about 5–7.5cm. Heat the oil in a large, wide frying pan and brown the onions. Add the meat and brown in several batches, adding more oil if needed. Transfer to a flameproof casserole.

2 Tip out the excess fat from the frying pan and pour in the wine and vinegar. Bring to the boil, scraping in all the brown residues on the base of the pan. Pour over the meat and onions in the casserole.

3 Add the remaining ingredients and enough water to cover. Bring to the boil, turn the heat down, cover, and simmer gently for 2 hours until the meat is tender, stirring occasionally.

4 Uncover the casserole and raise the heat slightly, letting it bubble for a further 30 minutes or so, stirring from time to time, to reduce the sauce slightly; skim any fat off the surface, then taste and adjust seasoning.

Ingredients

1.5kg chuck steak, trimmed
85ml virgin olive oil
1.5kg pickling onions, or small shallots, skinned
150ml red wine
3 tbsp red wine vinegar
3 garlic cloves, chopped
2 bay leaves
2 cinnamon sticks
3 tbsp tomato purée
salt and freshly ground black pepper

Tools

Sharp knife
Cutting board
Large frying pan
Large flameproof casserole
Ladle

lamb tava with cumin and mixed beans

This Greek-Cypriot style dish is named after the pot in which it is cooked, a *tava* or unglazed terracotta casserole. Originally, the *tava* was cooked on glowing wood embers, dug into the earth. Nowadays, it is slow cooked in the oven to a melting tenderness.

Serves 4
Preparation Time: 2 hours 10 minutes

Method

1   Preheat the oven to 150°C/Gas 2. Heat the oil in the ovenproof casserole, when hot, add the onions, and fry until golden before adding the seasoned lamb cubes. Fry until the lamb is browned all over, about 8–10 minutes.

2   Pour the white wine over and cook for a further 5 minutes until the wine is reduced in volume, add the tomatoes, bay leaf and spices; pour the stock over and bring to the boil. Cover with a tight fitting lid and place in the oven for 1½ hours.

3   Cook the French beans in boiling salted water, until just tender; remove with a slotted spoon into a bowl of cold water to refresh. Repeat with the yellow wax beans. Boil the broad beans for 2–3 minutes. Refresh in cold water. Drain the vegetables and dry them. Remove the skins of the broad beans.

4   Remove the lamb from the oven and add the beans. Return to the oven for a further 10 minutes before serving.

Ingredients

3 tbsp virgin olive oil
400g button onions or
    2 onions, thinly sliced
4 x 175g trimmed lamb
    rumps, cut into 4cm
    cubes
salt and freshly ground
    black pepper
150ml dry white wine
450g tomatoes, skinned,
    peeled, roughly
    chopped
1 bay leaf
2 tsp cumin seeds
½ tsp ground cinnamon
450ml meat stock or
    water

200g French beans,
    trimmed
100g yellow wax beans,
    trimmed
150g broad beans

Tools

Ovenproof casserole
    with lid
Saucepan
Slotted spoon
Bowl

chicken mousaka

The head chef at the internationally renowned Annabelle Hotel in Paphos for some 22 years, polycarpos demetriou serves his much acclaimed Cypriot food to a discerning clientèle. He has kindly allowed me to use his recipe for Chicken Mousaka which I am sure you will enjoy.

Serves 2
Preparation Time: 45 minutes

Method

1 Preheat the grill to its highest setting. Preheat the oven to 190°C/Gas 5. Brush a medium size ovenproof dish with a little olive oil. Heat a large frying pan until hot, add the olive oil, and onions and fry for 5 minutes until softened. Add the chicken and fry for 3–4 minutes until browned and just cooked. Add the chopped tomatoes, parsley and oregano, and season with salt and pepper. Cook for 3-4 minutes and remove from the heat.

2 Layer the potato slices in the ovenproof dish and season with salt, pepper and dried mint. Sprinkle over 1 tbsp of the haluomi cheese, layer the aubergine slices, and repeat with the seasoning and more cheese.

3 Spoon over the chicken mixture and press down to flatten slightly. Layer in the courgette and tomato slices, seasoning and adding cheese between each layer.

4 Place the dish under the preheated grill for 5 minutes to dry out the tomatoes slightly. Spoon the béchamel sauce over the tomatoes to cover, then sprinkle the remaining haloumi cheese over. Place in the oven for 15 minutes until golden brown and hot. Serve hot with a Greek salad.

Ingredients

olive oil for brushing
1 tsp virgin olive oil
90g onions, chopped
225g chicken breasts, skin removed, minced
250g tomatoes, skinned, seeded, chopped
3 tbsp chopped fresh flat-leaf parsley
1 tsp dried oregano
salt and freshly ground black pepper
4 small potatoes, sliced and deep fried
1 tbsp dried mint
6 tbsp grated haloumi cheese
1 small aubergine, sliced and chargrilled
1 small courgette, sliced and chargrilled
200g tomatoes, skinned, thinly sliced
450ml prepared béchamel white sauce

Tools

Brush
Ovenproof baking dish
Large frying pan
Large spoon

chicken with honey

Serves 4
Preparation Time:
2 hours 25 minutes

Ingredients

salt and ground
  white pepper
4 large whole leg
  portions of chicken
  (about 1kg)
¼ tsp saffron threads,
  roughly crushed
900g tomatoes, peeled,
  coarsely chopped
½ medium onion, finely
  chopped
1 tsp finely chopped
  ginger root
50g unsalted butter
3 tbsp honey
½ tsp ground cinnamon
1 tbsp groundnut oil
50g whole blanched
  almonds
2 tsp sesame seeds,
  toasted

Tools

2 deep casseroles with
  lids
Wooden spoon
Small frying pan

'Sofra' has held its place as one of the great Turkish restaurants in London for many years. Its owner, huseyin ozer, is a passionate man, whose sole aim in life is to provide the traditional taste of Turkish cooking and traditional hospitality.

Method

1 Preheat the oven to 240°C/Gas 9. Season the chicken well and rub the saffron into the skin. Arrange it in a single layer in deep casserole. Add the tomatoes, onion, ginger and butter. Cover and cook in the oven for 10 minutes; reduce the heat to 180°C/Gas 4 and cook for about 2 hours, testing for doneness after 1 hour.
2 Remove the chicken, transfer it to a clean casserole and set aside. Return the first casserole to a very high heat and boil the tomato mixture rapidly for about 10 minutes or until it has reduced to a syrupy consistency.
3 Remove the tomato sauce from the heat. Stir in the honey and cinnamon and season to taste. Pour the sauce over the chicken. Cover the casserole and simmer on top of the stove, or put in a medium oven, for a few minutes. Just before serving, heat the groundnut oil in a small pan, sauté the almonds briefly then scatter the almonds and sesame seeds over the casserole.

coffee and tea

The people of the Balkans take their coffee and tea drinking very seriously. The coffee in general is thick and sweet while the tea is light and fragrant although there are obviously some exceptions. Some Greeks believe that there are at least fifty ways to flavour coffee, while most will chose between *metrio* 'with some sugar' and *glyko* – 'sweet'. Many of the teas drunk in this region are made from herbal infusions and also often sweetened with honey.

5 Tea pot Tea in the Balkans is not served with milk, but made as a quite weak infusion. This tall pot allows the herbs to swirl about in the boiling water and then settle to the bottom before the tea is served. The long curved spout means that the tea can easily be poured, often from quite a height, into the glasses and then serve perhaps with a slice of lemon or a spoon of honey.

1 Briki A long handled coffee pot usually made of brass and almost always ornately decorated. As the pot is placed over direct heat the long handle enables the pot to be carried and poured with ease. There is a broad lip that is tapered towards the top so the coffee can be poured into the small cups.

2 Coffee cups Since the coffee in the Balkans is drunk very strong, very hot and usually very sweet, it is served in rather small cups. They have no handles but are again ornately decorated.

3 Coffee pot On more formal occasions the coffee is not made in the pot but in another vessel and then poured into a serving pot such as this. The handle is made of the same material as the pot, but again the spout is long and narrows to a point to fit into the small cups.

4 Tea glasses These beautifully decorated little glasses are tougher than they look. Made of quite thin glass they are able to take the steaming infusions made from mint, camomile or sage.

eastern mediterranean

eastern mediterranean
lebanon, syria and israel

The cooking of Lebanon and Syria is closely intertwined. These relatively new nations, strategically placed between East and West, share a joint history of invasion by the Persians, Greeks, Romans, Turks and French, all of whom left their mark on the cuisine. For centuries they were part of the Ottoman Empire and it is the Turkish influence that is most immediately apparent: grilled meats and meatballs; dips made of pulses, nuts and yogurt; stuffed vegetables; bulghur dishes and rice pilafs; plus the rich, syrupy pastries that are a hallmark of this region. After the First World War, the Ottoman Empire was dismantled and the French stepped in. In just twenty-five years they too had a tremendous impact on the local cuisine, giving it a new refinement and delicacy and stimulating the growth of the local restaurant trade, which helped to turn cities like Beirut into fashionable resorts.

It would be wrong, however, to consider Lebanese and Syrian food as merely a melting pot of other cuisines. It has marked traits that distinguish it from its Mediterranean neighbours, and a singular freshness that is evident in its vibrant salads such as *tabbouleh* (made with bulghur wheat) and *fattoush* (made with toasted stale bread), which are enlivened by masses of fresh herbs, such as mint, parsley, coriander and spring onions, plus a bracing seasoning of lemon juice.

Key ingredients of the region are wheat, rice, olives, nuts, tahini, fish, lamb, chicken, vegetables and fruit. These are staples throughout the Arab world but in Lebanon and Syria they are spiced up with tart or pungent flavours: lemon, yogurt, sumac (a lemon-tasting red berry that is dried and ground) and pomegranate molasses, a tangy syrup used with fish, meat, salads and vegetable dishes or served as a drink. Although flavours are distinctive, it is not a fiery cuisine. Instead there is a preference for warm spices, such as cinnamon, allspice and cumin. Tahini, an oily sesame seed paste, makes its way into dips, sauces and vegetable dishes. *Za'atar*, a mixture of thyme, sumac and sesame seeds, is used for dipping, with bread dunked first into olive oil and then into the dry mixture. Yogurt is still made in many homes, then used as a refreshing side dish, as the basis for sauces, or strained through muslin to make *labneh*, a soft, creamy cheese.

Wheat is an essential part of the diet – first as flour, to make the wonderful flatbreads, pittas and sesame-seed rings of the region; secondly steamed, dried and ground to make bulghur. Mixed with yogurt, then fermented and dried, bulghur wheat becomes *kishik*, a speciality of the region which is used to thicken soups and stews or served for breakfast. Bulghur is also an indispensable ingredient in the national dish of Lebanon and Syria – *kibbeh*. It is pounded to a smooth paste with onions, lamb, spices and herbs, traditionally in a large mortar and pestle, then shaped into patties and fried. There are hundreds of ways of preparing it. Sometimes the mixture is shaped round a filling of minced meat. It

ABOVE: 1 dried pomegranate seeds 2 cumin seeds 3 za'atar 4 sumac 5 tahini 6 dried spearmint (on the stem) 7 dried spearmint (crushed leaves)
OPPOSITE: 1 aubergines 2 radishes 3 fresh coriander 4 apricots 5 globe artichokes 6 courgette 7 chard 8 *labneh* balls in oil 9 flat-leaf parsley

can also be baked in a round tin to make *kibbeh saniyeh* or, in Syria, roasted on skewers with vegetables.

Although Lebanon and Syria have so many dishes in common, the preparation frequently varies from one country to the other. Lebanese cuisine is lighter, using less fat, and also produces more vegetarian dishes. Some areas of Syria have a

ABOVE: 1 olives 2 pine nuts 3 faraykee 4 semolina 5 molohia (dried spinach) 6 chickpeas

preference for spicy food, particularly the northern city of Aleppo, which is famed for its gastronomy, and also for the fiery Aleppo pepper.

One area for which both countries receive equal acclaim is their *mezze* table – a glorious array of little dishes that epitomises the generosity of the cooking of this region. Despite the simplicity of the dishes, there is always an innate sense of harmony and balance: earthy purées such as hummus and *baba ghanoush* (roasted aubergine); colourful salads, such as the refreshing *tabbouleh*; *sambousik* – crisp little crescent-shaped fritters filled with cheese and mint or spiced meat; neatly rolled vine leaves with a

filling of rice or meat; spicy sausages and meatballs; plus a vast array of shiny, plump, black and green olives and pickled vegetables. And there are always thin sheets of warm, fresh flatbreads stacked high. It's an assortment of colours, tastes and textures that cannot be bettered.

A *mezze* selection might be followed by a huge platter of grilled meats, served with one of the sauces of the region, such as *muhammara* (ground walnuts with chilli, red pepper and garlic), tarator (ground almonds or pine nuts mixed to a loose paste with breadcrumbs, lemon juice, garlic and water), or tahini mixed with lemon juice and garlic. Desserts are simple – seasonal fruits, baklavas, milky puddings flavoured with mastic or flower waters, or ice creams.

Like Lebanon and Syria, Israel has an ancient history but is a creation of the twentieth century. Unlike its neighbours, however, it has undergone a huge influx of immigrants, as Jews from all over the world flocked to the new nation state. Each brought their own culinary customs, and these were as varied as the countries they had left. Both the Ashkenazic and the Sephardic strands of Jewish cooking can be found in Israel – the former being primarily the cold-weather food of northern and eastern Europe, while the latter refers to the Jews of the Iberian peninsula. Yet the food of Israel can hardly be described as Jewish. There are also Palestinians, Christians and other minority groups, all of whom have different dietary traditions. The unifying factor is the heavy Arab influence, resulting in a cuisine rich in dairy products, pulses, wheat, nuts, fruit, lamb and vegetables.

Out of this culinary confusion, Israel is tentatively beginning to develop a national cuisine. It includes not only Mediterranean specialities such as hummus, falafel, meatballs and little savoury pies but also fresh salads, lots of raw vegetables such as cucumbers and avocados, citrus fruits and dairy produce. And, of course, there is an overlay of Jewish festival food, dishes from all parts of the world that have been eaten for centuries to celebrate religious holidays.

The Middle East is home to a myriad of religions and this is reflected in its cuisine. The traditions are eagerly passed down in this family-based society, the home cooking being where you will often find the best food. Family ties are very strong in all these countries, with the women still often staying home to care for the family. Thus the daughters, in their own kitchens, learn recipes from their mothers, aunts and grandmothers and then go on to add their own touches thus carry on this great food culture.

vegetable preparation tools

Well-made tools that sit comfortably in your hands are the best way to improve your cooking. With just a few key items you can prepare almost any type of vegetable, fruit, meat, fish or fowl. These tools then need to be looked after and sharpened regularly so that they last for years and years. Some vegetables as well as fruits need the simplest of preparation; peas just need removing from their pods while all redcurrants need is the remove of their stalks. Others, however, need a little more work to bring out their best.

1 Vegetable knife The curved end of the knife around to the tip is very useful and enables you to cut out blemishes from vegetables. The short length of the blade makes this knife ideal for cutting or peeling. A really sharp blade will enable you to slice through soft vegetables such as ripe tomatoes without damaging the flesh.

2 Paring knife This is very much like a small version of the universally useful cook's knife, but with a blade only 8–10cm long. It is very good for peeling, paring, scraping and slicing small vegetables. When it comes to chopping small amounts of garlic or ginger this smaller knife is perfect.

3 Man'ara This tool is basically like a very long apple corer which is great for hollowing our long vegetables as well as fruit, for example with the courgettes to be stuffed on page 94. The rounded end of the blade makes the initial piercing of the skin much easier while the narrowness of the curved blade leaves a pretty pattern on the vegetables or fruit.

4 Vegetable peeler This is the deluxe version of the standard vegetable peeler. It has short blade on the outside of the peeler area so that there is no need to use a knife as well when peeling and cutting something. There is also a guard to stop the blade from slipping on the vegetable or fruit and cutting your hand.

5 Vegetable peeler The fixed blade on this peeler can be used from both sides making it useable for both left- and right-handed people. The pointed end to the tool acts as another blade, which can be used to gouge out potato eyes or other blemishes.

stuffed courgettes with yogurt sauce
mehshi koossa bil laban

Stuffing vegetables is a pastime in the Middle East; they are generally filled with meat and vegetables, often including rice and pine nuts, and served at large family events. Courgettes and aubergines are scooped out using a special corer called a *man'ara*, rather like an apple corer, which does the job perfectly. This recipe is from the author and journalist, anissa helou, who was born and educated in Beirut. She has a serious interest in the food of the Levant and the culinary traditions of the Mediterranean.

Serves 4
Preparation Time: I hour

Ingredients

1.2kg small courgettes, about 20
125g short grain rice
200g minced fatty lamb
2 tbsp meat stock or water
¼ tsp ground cinnamon
½ tsp ground allspice
salt
¼ tsp finely ground black pepper

For the yogurt sauce

25g unsalted butter
½ bunch fresh coriander (100g), finely chopped
7 large garlic cloves, crushed
1kg thick set yogurt
1 egg, whisked

Tools

Sharp knife
Apple corer (or *man'ara*)
Bowl
2 large pans
Wooden spoon
Measuring jug

Method

1 First prepare the courgettes: cut off and discard the stem ends of the courgettes, dip the cut tops in a little salt to soften the pulp and make coring easier. Place a courgette in the palm of your hand with the cut top facing you. Hold it firmly and insert a Lebanese corer (*man'ara*) or apple corer into the cut top and as close to the edge as possible, about 2–3mm inside the skin. Then push half way down the courgette, take out and insert again next to the first incision, repeat until you cut all around the inside (*1*). Twirl the corer inside the courgette to loosen the pulp. When the pulp is completely extracted, plunge the cored courgettes in bowl of cold water to soak while you prepare the stuffing (*2*).

2 For the stuffing, wash the rice in 2–3 changes of water, drain and place in a mixing bowl. Add the meat, stock or water; season with cinnamon, allspice, salt and pepper and mix well.

3 Stuff the courgettes half full with the stuffing. Arrange with open end up, in a pan where they fit comfortably standing up; add 600ml water, cover, place on a high heat and simmer for 25 minutes.

4 Meanwhile, make the yogurt sauce: melt the butter in a frying pan over a medium heat, add the chopped coriander and garlic and cook for 1 minute, then remove from the heat. Put the yogurt in a large heavy saucepan, add the whisked egg and mix well with a wooden spoon and place over a medium heat; gently bring to the boil, stirring constantly with a wooden spoon in the same direction otherwise the yogurt will curdle. Simmer gently for 3 minutes still stirring.

5 Carefully remove the courgettes from the pan and add to the yogurt sauce. Measure 200ml of the courgette stock, gently stir into the simmering yogurt, and simmer uncovered for 10 minutes. Leave to sit for a few minutes, taste, adjust the seasoning and serve hot.

1

2

salmon kibbeh nayeh with soft herb salad

It is said that the Syrian women are the best *kibbeh* makers – with recipes handed down from generation to generation. *Kibbeh* is basically powdered meat mixed with burghul wheat, either served fried in balls (*kibbeh ras*), baked in a tray (*kibbeh sanieh*) or raw (*kibbeh nayeh*). This recipe is a modern variation on *kibbeh nayeh*, but unusual as salmon is unknown in the Middle East. It comes courtesy of greg malouf, one of Australia's most talented and well known chefs, born to Lebanese parents, who has drawn inspiration from his childhood memories and his travels throughout the Middle East.

Serves 6
Preparation Time: 10 minutes

Ingredients
300g fresh salmon, finely minced and chilled
2 shallots, finely chopped
150g burghul, white fine grade, soaked for 8 minutes in 150ml of water, then squeezed dry
⅓ tsp allspice
1 small red chilli, seeded, finely chopped
1 tsp salt
freshly ground black pepper
1 tbsp extra virgin olive oil
250g natural yogurt (hung in a cloth for 24–36 hours, see Note right)
½ garlic clove, crushed

For the salad
4 preserved baby artichokes in oil
50g mixed fresh coriander, mint and flat-leaf parsley, torn
1 red onion, finely sliced
juice of ½ lemon
100ml extra virgin olive oil
1 tsp sumac

Tools
3 bowls

Method
1 Chill a stainless steel bowl or glass bowl. Mix the salmon, shallots, burghul, allspice, chilli, salt and pepper with 1 tbsp of olive oil; form the mixture into 6 disc shapes and refrigerate.
2 In another bowl, blend the yogurt cheese and garlic.
3 Remove the leaves from the artichokes, keep the hearts for another use. In a third bowl, make the salad: mix the herb leaves, artichoke leaves, onion, lemon juice and 50ml of olive oil, season to taste.
4 To serve, place a disc of salmon *kibbeh* in the centre of each plate, place a dollop of yogurt cheese on the salmon *kibbeh*, and then top with a small amount of salad leaves. Drizzle the remaining oil around the salmon and sprinkle with the sumac.

Note
To hang the yogurt, simply place the yogurt in cheesecloth or thin muslin, tie up and hang above a bowl for a few hours; this gives you a richer and more concentrated product, known as *labneh* or yogurt-cheese.

grinding spices

Spices form the basis for most of the flavouring in Middle Eastern food. They are prized ingredients and often command high prices. For this reason they are used carefully and treated with respect. Unlike our Western supermarkets where herbs and spices are sold ready-ground or prepared in neat little jars, the markets of Israel, Syria and Lebanon are studded with stalls selling vast baskets or bowls of whole spices. These are then ground at home when they are about to be used – lengthening the life of the spice and increasing its flavour in the food.

1 Wooden mortar and pestle This tall mortar is made of smooth wood with very light grooves on the interior which can grind a variety of items including those with moisture. It is wider at the base than the top making it easier to grind vigorously with the pestle without spilling the contents.

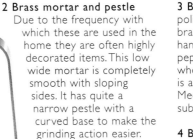

1

2

3

2 Brass mortar and pestle Due to the frequency with which these are used in the home they are often highly decorated items. This low wide mortar is completely smooth with sloping sides. It has quite a narrow pestle with a curved base to make the grinding action easier.

3 Brass pepper mill Made of polished and highly decorated brass, this pepper mill has its own handle, which is turned to grind the pepper rather than turning the whole top of the mill. Black pepper is a key spice in Eastern Mediterranean cookery used for its subtle flavour as well as for its heat.

4 Blender When you need to grind a large quantity of spices or they are particularly hard, this is your best tool. It has a very powerful motor with a sharp two-armed blade that can handle just about everything. You have to make sure that it is scrupulously clean both before and after using it for spices so you do not add any unwanted flavour to any other foods.

5 Coffee mill This is effectively a smaller version of the blender. The blade is the same shape but the motor will be less powerful and it only holds a relatively small amount. As with the blender it is important that it is thoroughly cleaned before and after if you use the same machine for grinding coffee. If you plan to grind a lot of spices it is worth buying another mill to be used solely for spices.

4

5

hot and sweet red pepper dip with walnuts and pomegranate

This wonderful hot pepper dip is from paula wolfert, the noted food writer based in San Francisco whose knowledge of the Eastern Mediterranean is legendary. This popular *mezze* style dip is a speciality of Gazlantep in southeast Turkey, and also in Syria: in both countries it is called 'Muhammara'. In some regions it may include sesame seed paste instead of walnuts. Paula's version is wonderful, it is great served with kebabs, grilled meats and fish. I also enjoy it just simply spread on toast.

Makes 750ml
Preparation Time: 15 minutes plus 8 hours chilling

Tools
Cooling rack
Blender/ food processor

Ingredients
6–8 red peppers,
   (about 1kg), roasted,
   peeled, seeded,
   membranes removed
150g coarsely ground
   walnuts
50g crumbled unsalted
   crackers
2 tbsp pomegranate
   molasses
1 tbsp lemon juice
½ tsp ground cumin, plus
   a pinch
½ tsp caster sugar
¾ tsp salt
3 tbsp olive oil
2 hot red chillies,
   roasted, peeled,
   seeded, membranes
   removed
2 tbsp pine nuts, roasted

Method
1 Spread the red peppers, skin side up, on paper towels on a cooling rack and drain for about 10 minutes.
2 In a blender or food processor, combine the walnuts, crackers, pomegranate molasses, lemon juice, cumin, sugar and salt, and purée until creamy. With the motor running, add 2 tbsp of the oil in a thin stream. Add the chillies. If the dip seems too thick, thin it with 1–2 tbsp of water. Transfer to a non-reactive container, cover and refrigerate for at least 8 hours.
3 Place the dip in a serving dish, sprinkle with the pine nuts and the pinch of cumin. Drizzle with the remaining 1 tbsp of oil.

musakhan chicken

Musakhan chicken is a Palestinian speciality, chicken cooked with onion, cinnamon and sumac, then wrapped inside *shirak*, the Israeli flatbread. Pitta breads or *khoubz* makes a very respectable substitute.

Serves 4
Preparation Time: 30 minutes

Ingredients

3 tbsp olive oil
salt and freshly ground
    black pepper
4 x 170g skinless,
    boneless chicken
    breasts
2 onions, sliced
1 tsp ground cinnamon
2 tsp sumac
600ml chicken stock
juice of ½ lemon

50g pine nuts, toasted
2 tbsp chopped fresh
    coriander
4 pitta breads or *shirak*

Tools

Frying pan
Knife
Cutting board
Bowl

Method

1 Heat the oil in a frying pan, season the chicken and add to the pan; cook for 1–2 minutes until golden. Remove to one side.

2 Add the onions to the pan, cook for 5–10 minutes until golden, then add the cinnamon and sumac. Return the chicken to the pan, pour the stock over, and bring to the boil; cook for 5 minutes.

3 Remove and cut up the chicken into bite size pieces; place in a bowl and squeeze over the lemon juice. Add the pine nuts and coriander.

4 Cut the pitta breads in half lengthways, fill with the chicken and pan juices. Serve with a light salad.

baking and serving dishes

Much of the cooking of the Eastern Mediterranean involves the slow cooking of meats and vegetables to blend the many spices and flavourings that are traditional. Sometimes the baking dishes used are covered ceramic pots but in many cases they are made from metal so that the initial cooking can be done over direct heat. Many of the recipes are served in their cooking dishes but others are transferred to ornately decorated metal platters that can hold hot and cold food alike. These vary in size from the size of a side plate up to a huge platter suitable for a crowd.

1 Sorj This is a Lebanese cooking dish that was traditionally found in every home kitchen. The single handle on this older version serves two purposes; firstly so it can be hung on a wall or above the stove and also so it is easier to handle.

2 Sorj The name of this concave dish comes from the bread, which was traditionally cooked in it. This *sorj* is a modern one with riveted handles on each side so it can easily be removed from the heat. The curved base and sides are perfect for creating domed breads, which puff up when hot.

3 Sanieh This is the term for the beaten metal cooking or serving platters of Lebanon and Syria. This one is quite a modern type with the decoration kept to a minimum. It could be used for serving *tageen samak* (baked fish).

4 Old sanieh The intricately etched decoration on this older *sanieh* shows that it was probably hand made. The food can be served directly on the plate but these dishes are also used as serving trays for cups or tea glasses. They are kept highly polished in the home.

5 Large sanieh You can see from this *sanieh* just how large they can be. A *sanieh* like this would be used when entertaining a large group. It might be filled with *falafel* or other Middle Eastern *meze* either as a snack to eat with drinks or as part of a lengthy meal.

pitta bread
khoubz arabieh

'Khoubz Arabieh' is the term for Arabic style flatbreads. They are great for holding fillings such as kebabs, or to dip sauces such as *hummus* and *besira*. This bread is usually cooked in the communal wood-fired oven that can reach extremely high temperatures, and which is found in most towns and villages. Ensure you have your oven set at the highest possible setting for the best result.

Makes 8 pittas
Preparation Time: 1 hour plus 1 hour 30 minutes proving

Ingredients
25g fresh yeast
pinch of sugar
400ml warm water
450g plain flour plus
    extra for dusting
½ tsp salt
sunflower oil for greasing

Tools
3 bowls
2 teacloths
Brush
3 large baking sheets
Rolling pin
Cooling rack

Method
1 In a bowl, mix the yeast with the sugar and 4 tbsp of the water, leave the liquid to become bubbly, about 10–15 minutes. Mix the flour and salt in a mixing bowl, make a well in the centre, add the yeast mixture and then work into a dough with the remaining water to a firm consistency, knead for 10 minutes.
2 When the dough is smooth and pliable, shape into a ball, place in a lightly greased bowl, cover with clingfilm or a damp teacloth and set aside in a warm place for 1–1½ hours or until doubled in volume (1 opposite).
3 Preheat the oven to 260°C/Gas 9 or highest setting. Turn out the dough on to a floured surface. Punch down the dough, then divide into 8 equal portions. Roll each portion into a ball, dust with flour, place on a board, cover with a dry teacloth and prove for a further 15 minutes (2 opposite).
4 Grease 3 large baking sheets lightly with oil, place in the hot oven for 5 minutes. Roll out each ball of dough on a floured surface with a floured rolling pin to a rough circle about 15cm diamete (3 opposite). Transfer 2 or 3 at a time to a hot baking sheet. Cook in the oven for about 6 minutes until puffed up but still quite pale in colour. Repeat with the remaining pittas, cooking them a few at a time.
5 Place on a cooling rack, then cover with a teacloth to keep them soft.

Tarator

Tarator is a powerful, robust garlicky sauce based on tahini (sesame seed paste), popular throughout the Eastern Mediterranean. It is especially good as a dip for the warm *khoubz*, served alongside cold fish and vegetables.

Ingredients
2 slices white bread,
    soaked in water, then
    squeezed
4 garlic cloves, peeled
    and chopped
1 tsp salt
120g tahini
juice of ½ lemon
3 tbsp chopped fresh
    flat-leaf parsley

Method
Place the bread, garlic, salt and tahini in a small blender and whiz briefly to blend. Drizzle in the lemon juice. Thin to a consistency of a dip with a little warm water, stir in the parsley and serve.

moulds and cutters

Like many cultures, the Middle East has a wealth of different finger foods. Some of these are cut to size but many of them are moulded – making them easy to pick up and pop in the mouth. Often these foods have their own traditional shape that makes them instantly recognisable. Some of the tools compress the ingredient mixtures into a plain shape while others have the added function of embossing a pattern at the same time. Here we have two extremes; from the shiny new metal tools to the old and slightly worn hand-made wooden ones.

1 **Falafel mould** The two parts of this mould work together. Firstly the cylindrical handled mould is held with the wide end at the top. The short lever is then pulled down and the *falafel* mixture popped inside. The trowel-like implement is used to smooth the mixture across the top and finally the lever is released to form a perfect round, flat *falafel*

2,3,4,5 **Tabi (or taabeh) moulds to make ma'amoul** The Easter sweets are made using tools such as these. They are all of varying sizes, patterns and shapes but are used in the same way. The dough-like mixture is pressed into them and then turned out on to a baking sheet for baking. The carved wooden handles make the whole process much easier.

small savoury lebanese pastries

In the Middle East, *meze* often includes small savoury pastries, made of different style pastry doughs filled with cheese, meat, vegetables or fish. Now due to the availability of filo pastry in the Middle East, it is much more widely used in making these delicate filled pastries. Delicious as party food, served freshly baked, or great for a snack at any time.

minced lamb rolls (lahm bi'ajeen)

These can be also known as Ladies' Fingers – they are rolled like oriental spring rolls, filled with spiced lamb. Remember filo quickly dries out and becomes difficult to work.

Makes 16 rolls
Preparation time: 55 minutes

Ingredients	Tools
2 tbsp virgin olive oil	Frying pan
2 tbsp pine nuts, chopped	Slotted spoon
300g finely minced lamb	Wooden spoon
1 onion, finely chopped	Bowl
salt and freshly ground black pepper	Sharp knife
½ tsp ground cumin	Pastry brush
½ tsp ground allspice	Baking sheets
1 tbsp tamarind paste	
3 tbsp chopped fresh mint	
4 sheets filo pastry	
40g unsalted butter, melted	

Method

1 Heat the oil in a frying pan, add the pine nuts, cook until golden, then remove with a slotted spoon. Return the pan to a high heat.
2 Add the lamb, cook for 8–10 minutes until sealed and golden Add the onion, seasoning and spices. Stir in the tamarind paste, the mint and the pine nuts. Place in a bowl and allow to go cold.
3 Preheat oven to 190°C/Gas 5. Cut each filo sheet into 4 rectangles 20cm x 13cm, pile them on top of each other and cover with a damp cloth.
4 Brush one sheet liberally with melted butter. Take a good spoonful of filling and place at one end of the strip. Roll up the strip to enclose the filling, then turn in the sides, and roll up like a spring roll. Prepare all 16 strips the same way.
5 Place on a baking sheet, brush with butter and bake for 10–15 minutes until crisp and golden.

Fattayer

You can prepare fattayer using the same lamb filling, wrapped in sambousik pastry (see right), made into tiny triangles. Simply roll out the dough and cut out 12cm diameter circles, using a cookie cutter. Fill the centre of each dough circle with the lamb and then bring up the dough on all three sides, meeting at the top; pinch together with your fingers to close. Brush with beaten eggs and place on a baking sheet, bake for 20–25 minutes until golden.

sambousik

Sambousik are small crescent-shaped pastries: my particular favourite is a filling of chopped spinach with cheese and eggs. They make great cocktail canapés. Traditionally the pastry would be shaped and flattened by hand, but using a cookie cutter is easier.

Makes 20
Preparation time: 50 minutes

Ingredients	Tools
50g unsalted butter	Small saucepan
120ml virgin olive oil	2 bowls
1 tsp salt	Sharp knife
450g plain flour	Chopping board
little beaten egg, to glaze	Frying pan
	Spoon
	Rolling pin
	Cookie cutter
	Baking sheet
	Pastry brush

For the filling
10g unsalted butter
2 tbsp olive oil
1 onion, finely chopped
400g fresh spinach, chopped
100g feta cheese, crumbled
2 hard-boiled eggs, diced

Method

1 Preheat the oven to 190°C/Gas 5. For the pastry, melt the butter in a small pan, and pour into a bowl. Add the oil, 120ml water and salt, and stir well. Add the flour a little at a time, mixing it in well until the pastry is smooth and pliable.
2 For the filling, heat a frying pan with the butter and olive oil, when hot add the onion, cook until softened. Add the spinach and cook for 3–4 minutes until no liquid comes from the spinach. Remove with a spoon. Place in a bowl, allow to go cold, add the cheese and the egg.
3 Roll out the dough then cut out 20 circles of 7.5cm diameter using a cookie cutter. Place the filling on one half of the circle, then fold over the other half, close to seal, then crimp the seal with your finger and thumb. Prepare all the sambousik the same way.
4 Place on a baking sheet, 5cm apart, brush with the beaten egg and bake for 20–25 minutes. Alternatively deep fry until golden and drain on kitchen paper. Sambousik are best served hot but can also be eaten cold.

mincing meat

The action of mincing meat not only changes the obvious size of the pieces of meat it also opens up possibilities of how you can prepare and cook it. By mincing different meats together you can cohesively combine flavours. The meat you use can be from cheaper cuts and you can combine it with vegetables, nuts, herbs and spices. By mincing your own meat at home you ensure that you know exactly what you are actually getting.

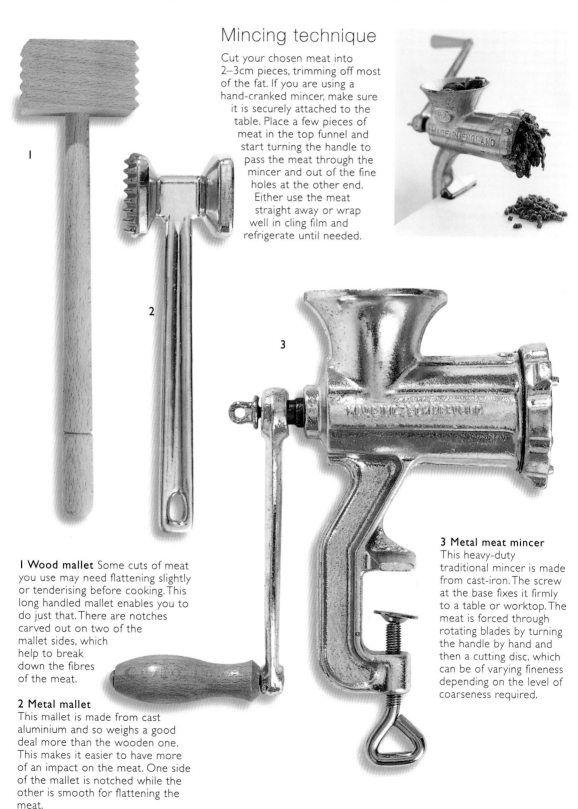

Mincing technique

Cut your chosen meat into 2–3cm pieces, trimming off most of the fat. If you are using a hand-cranked mincer, make sure it is securely attached to the table. Place a few pieces of meat in the top funnel and start turning the handle to pass the meat through the mincer and out of the fine holes at the other end. Either use the meat straight away or wrap well in cling film and refrigerate until needed.

I Wood mallet Some cuts of meat you use may need flattening slightly or tenderising before cooking. This long handled mallet enables you to do just that. There are notches carved out on two of the mallet sides, which help to break down the fibres of the meat.

2 Metal mallet
This mallet is made from cast aluminium and so weighs a good deal more than the wooden one. This makes it easier to have more of an impact on the meat. One side of the mallet is notched while the other is smooth for flattening the meat.

3 Metal meat mincer
This heavy-duty traditional mincer is made from cast-iron. The screw at the base fixes it firmly to a table or worktop. The meat is forced through rotating blades by turning the handle by hand and then a cutting disc, which can be of varying fineness depending on the level of coarseness required.

lebanese falafel with pomegranate spearmint dressing

Basic to many cuisines of the Middle East, *falafel* are made a little differently by every cook. They are said to have originated in Egypt, where they are called *tameya*, and are made with plump dried broad beans, spiced then deep fried until golden. This recipe is traditionally Israeli and Lebanese in make up, and is made using dried chickpeas, although some recipes call for a mixture of both. Dried spearmint and pomegranate molasses (*dibs rumen*) are available in Middle Eastern stores.

Serves 10 (makes 20 *falafel*)
Preparation Time: 2 hours 10 minutes, plus overnight soaking

Ingredients
450g dried chickpeas, soaked overnight
90g bulghur wheat, soaked overnight
1 onion, very finely chopped
6 garlic cloves, crushed
4 spring onions, very finely chopped
1 large bunch flat-leaf parsley, chopped
1 large bunch fresh coriander, chopped
2 tsp ground cumin
1 tsp ground coriander
1 tsp baking soda
salt and freshly ground black pepper, pinch of cayenne, pinch of turmeric
vegetable oil for deep frying

For the dressing
1 tbsp pomegranate molasses
2 tsp dried spearmint
1 garlic clove, crushed
4 tomatoes, seeded, cut into 0.5cm dice
¼ cucumber, cut into 0.5cm dice
juice of 2 lemons
120ml virgin olive oil
¼ tsp dried red chilli flakes
2 tbsp chopped fresh coriander

Tools
Blender
2 bowls
Fryer or large saucepan
Abel falafel (falafel mould)
Slotted spoon

Method
1 Drain the chickpeas, then place in a blender or food processor, whiz to a smooth paste (the texture should be very smooth).
2 Transfer to a bowl, all the remaining ingredients except the vegetable oil. Mix well, cover, leave in the refrigerator for 2 hours.
3 Heat the vegetable oil in a fryer or large pan to 180°C.
4 Wet your hands, shape the chickpea mixture into 20 balls of 4cm diameter, then flatten them lightly into small cubes. Traditionally a *falafel* mould (*abel falafel*) would be used to help shape them.
5 Working in batches, fry the *falafel* in hot oil for 3–4 minutes until golden, remove with a slotted spoon, drain on kitchen paper, and keep warm.
6 In a bowl, mix all the dressing ingredients together and season to taste. Serve the *falafel* on a bed of *tehinah* (see note below), topped with a little of the pomegranate dressing.

Note
Every vendor in the Middle East serves his *falafel* with a selection of accompaniments, including *tehinah* (sesame seed sauce). It is easy to make – it should not be too fluid, but not too thick either, with a good balance of acidity and garlicky flavours. To make it, simply take 120ml sesame seed paste (tahini), add 4 tbsp of water, juice of 1 lemon, 2 crushed garlic cloves, then season with a little cumin and paprika, stir well and serve.

Other traditional accompaniments include pickles, and a spicy chilli paste called *zhug*, a Yemenite speciality.

easter sweets
ma'amoul joz

These delicious little walnut-stuffed sweet cookies are made in the Lebanon at Easter time. They can be made of chopped pistachio or walnuts, even almonds, and they are traditionally flavoured with *mahlab*, a Syrian spice from the kernel of the cherry stone, both sweet and spicy with a vanilla like aroma. It is used to flavour breads such as *ka'ak*.

Makes 35–40 sweets
Preparation Time: 2 hours

Method

1 Preheat oven to 230°C/Gas 8. In a bowl combine the semolina, butter and sugar, rub together with your fingertips, and allow to rest for 1 hour. Warm the milk and pour into a bowl, add the yeast and, when bubbling, add the *mahlab*, then add to the semolina mixture. Add the rosewater.
2 Knead together for 2–3 minutes, then leave for a further 30 minutes; knead again for a final time to form a pliable dough.
3 For the filling, mix all the ingredients together.
4 Take a spoonful of the dough and shape it in your hand into a ball. Press the centre of the dough to make a hole, then fill with a generous amount of the nut filling, then mould the dough over the filling, flatten slightly with your hand. Bake on a greased baking sheet for 15 minutes. Traditionally you should press the filled ball on a special wooden mould (*tabi*), then tap out and bake.
5 When cooked, remove from the oven and place on a wire rack to cool. Dust with icing sugar, then store in an airtight container – if they last that long!

Ingredients

500g fine semolina
250g unsalted butter
½ tbsp caster sugar
5 tbsp full fat milk
1 tsp dried yeast
1 tsp *mahlab*
3 tbsp rosewater or
   orange flower water
icing sugar, to dust

For the filling

250g walnuts, finely
   ground
1 tbsp caster sugar
1 tbsp rosewater

Tools

2 bowls
Saucepan
Spoon
Wooden mould (*tabi*)
Baking tray
Cooling rack

casseroles and baking dishes

The baking dishes of the Middle East are often simple and unadorned, either made from beaten metal such as copper or chunky earthenware that is sometimes glazed. The earthenware or clay pots are some of the earliest and most basic types of cooking vessel that were originally used over an open fire. These have evolved over the centuries to our modern equivalents but the basic principles are the same. They are designed for gently simmering stews or moist dishes because they absorb the heat slowly and evenly and they have tight-fitting lids to prevent any steam escaping.

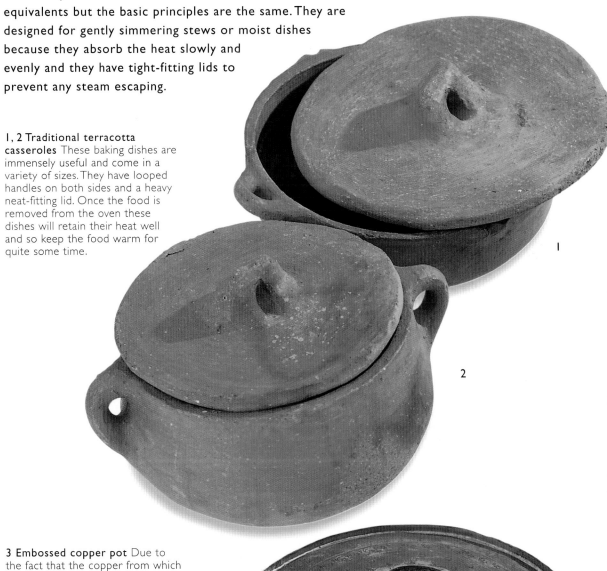

1, 2 Traditional terracotta casseroles These baking dishes are immensely useful and come in a variety of sizes. They have looped handles on both sides and a heavy neat-fitting lid. Once the food is removed from the oven these dishes will retain their heat well and so keep the food warm for quite some time.

3 Embossed copper pot Due to the fact that the copper from which this pot is made is quite thin, it conducts heat very quickly and is more suitable for shorter cooking times such as the baking of the rice and fish for *sayyadiyah*. It has no handles so a wide heatproof cloth is needed to bring it to the table.

baked fish

tageen samak

The internationally renowned cookery writer and best selling author claudia roden needs no introduction. Her books have brought the flavours of the Middle East to homes everywhere and she is generally credited with having introduced the western palate to Middle Eastern cuisine. This recipe for *tageen samak* (baked fish) is simple, healthy and full of heady aromas.

Serves 4
Preparation Time: 50 minutes

Ingredients
1.5kg firm white fish
   fillets
salt and freshly ground
   black pepper
olive or sunflower oil
juice of ½ lemon
2–4 garlic cloves, finely
   chopped
1kg tomatoes, peeled
   and chopped
2 tsp sugar (*optional*)
250g onions, finely sliced
2 tbsp blanched
   almonds, coarsely
   chopped or sliced
1½ tbsp raisins
large bunch of fresh flat-
   leaf parsley, deep fried
   in oil, to garnish
lemon slices, to garnish
   (*optional*)

Tools
1 large baking dish
2 frying pans

Method
1 Preheat oven to 200°C/Gas 6. Put the fillets in a baking dish in a single layer. Rub with salt, pepper and 2 tbsp oil and the lemon juice, cover with foil. Bake for 10–12 minutes or until the flesh becomes translucent and just begins to flake, keep warm.

2 Meanwhile, fry the garlic in 2 tbsp oil and as it begins to colour, add the tomatoes with a little sugar if they are not very sweet. Cook gently for 20 minutes or until the tomatoes reduce to a thick paste.

3 In another pan, fry the onions in 3 tbsp oil until golden. Add the almonds and raisins, fry until the almonds colour and the raisins puff up.

4 To serve, lay the fish on a large serving plate, pour the tomato sauce over and cover with the fried onion mixture. Garnish with the deep fried parsely, and lemon slices if you like.

fried fish with rice and caramelised onions
sayyadiyah

My first introduction into this impressive dish came many years ago while working at The Royal Garden Hotel in London. There we had an Egyptian chef from Cairo called Abdul who taught me how to make *sayyadiyah* along with many other Arabic specialities. It is usually made with whole fish; use white fish such as halibut, monkfish or turbot.

Serves 4
Preparation Time: 1 hour 10 minutes

Method

1 Heat 90ml of the oil in a pan, then add the onions, and fry slowly over a moderate heat until the onions are dark golden but not burnt, turning them regularly; about 20 minutes. Remove with a slotted spoon on to kitchen paper. When dry, grind the onions to a coarse powder in a mortar or small blender.
2 Return the cooking pan to the heat, add the ground onions, turmeric, coriander, cumin, salt and pepper. Add the fish stock and simmer for 15 minutes.
3 Preheat the oven to 200°C/Gas 6. Add the rice to the stock, return to the boil, reduce the heat and simmer for 20 minutes. Remove from the heat, leave to stand for 5 minutes covered with a lid.
4 Meanwhile, heat the remaining oil in a frying pan, add the seasoned fish fillets, cook for 2–3 minutes on each side until cooked and golden; remove with a fish slice.
5 To serve, place the fish in the base of a small deep casserole or 20cm tin, lightly greased with butter or oil. Pack the rice on top, pressing down well. Place in the oven for 10 minutes, then invert on to a serving dish, sprinkle the toasted pine nuts and chopped coriander over and garnish with lemon wedges.

Ingredients

120ml vegetable oil
4 large onions, thinly
  sliced
½ tsp ground turmeric
1 tsp ground coriander
1 tsp ground cumin
salt and freshly ground
  black pepper
700ml fish stock
400g long grain rice
800g white fish fillet, cut
  into 5cm chunks
butter or oil for greasing
50g pine nuts, toasted
3 tbsp chopped fresh
  coriander
lemon wedges, to serve

Tools

Large pan
Slotted spoon
Mortar and pestle or
  small blender
Frying pan
Fish slice
Deep casserole
  or 20cm tin

mahgreb and egypt

mahgreb and egypt

morocco, tunisia, algeria, libya and egypt

As with so many Mediterranean regions, it is possible to trace the history of the Mahgreb through the influences on its food. The name Mahgreb originates from the Arab word meaning 'unfamiliar' or 'remote'. To the seventh century Arab invaders from the East, this rugged, fertile, northwestern edge of Africa was indeed a strange and distant land. Bordered by mountains and desert on one side and the Mediterranean on the other, it has more in common with southern Europe than with the rest of Africa – both in terms of its climate and its cooking.

Over the course of 800 years, the Arabs left not only a linguistic and religious imprint on the Mahgreb but also a culinary one. Initially the Arab diet was simple, based on grains, grilled meats, vegetables and fruits – plus the nomad's staples of ewes' milk and dates – ingredients that form the backbone of the diet today. But as the Islamic Empire grew, it absorbed Persian culinary traditions: lavish, intricate dishes, meats marinated in yogurt, exotic spicing, fruit preserves, and the combination of sweet and savoury tastes.

The next culinary contribution came from the Turks, with the spread of the Ottoman Empire throughout northwest Africa from the sixteenth century onwards. Although in rural areas the peasant diet remained largely unchanged, in the towns and cities elaborate banquets were given in the Turkish style, often with guests numbering in their thousands. Kebabs and meatballs, stuffed vegetables, aromatic rice pilafs, and intricate pastries filled with nuts and laden with syrup all became part of the cuisine. Spain, France and Italy took over after the Turks moved out, and in the early twentieth century the big cities of the Mahgreb – Fez, Casablanca, Marrakech and Algiers – took on a European gloss, with many restaurants offering dual menus, and French refinements such as pastry-making and saucing taking hold.

Although the food of northwest Africa has many strands in common with the rest of the Mediterranean, it also has a unique character of its own. It is highly aromatic, perfumed with cinnamon, saffron, ginger, mint, coriander, citrus fruits and delicate flower waters such as orange, rose and jasmine. Meat and fish are cooked with dried fruits such as dates, prunes and apricots, or fresh ones such as quinces, to create *tagines* of great succulence and flavor, cooked in the earthenware pots of the same name with their distinctive conical lids. Hearty soups are a common feature throughout the region, often linked to religious rituals – the Moroccan *harira*, a thick bean and meat soup served at Ramadan, the *molokhia* of Egypt, made of the green leaves of the

same name, the *brudu* of Tunisia and the *chorba* of Algeria. Couscous – the name given to both the semolina granules and the fragrant stew with which they are served – has come to symbolise the cuisine of northwest Africa. Its character varies from country to country – and indeed from home to home. In Morocco it is a relatively light dish, often made with

ABOVE: 1 prunes 2 raisins 3 preserved lemons
4 couscous 5 dried broad beans 6 almonds
7 red lentils
OPPOSITE: 1 spinach 2 orange 3 lemon 4 okra
5 pomegranate 6 sweet red chillies 7 hot green chillies
8 fresh mint 9 fresh coriander

The cuisine of Morocco is the most sophisticated of the Mahgreb. Its strong Arab roots have developed into something completely original, and there is a lightness of touch to its spicing that can barely be equalled anywhere in the Mediterranean. Sometimes a single spice, such as cumin or cinnamon, is used in a dish; at other times many spices are added in tiny amounts to give a layering of flavors. The most famous Moroccan spice mix is *ras el hanout*, meaning 'top of the shop', and each spice merchant will have their own special blend, sometimes made up of over 20 different spices. *Chermoula* is a fragrant spice paste made of chilli, coriander, cumin, lemon juice and olive oil and used to marinate meat and fish. The tart, salty tang of preserved lemons is used to lift the flavors of meat and fish *tagines*. For refreshment, heavily sweetened mint tea is served.

Tunisia, Algeria and Libya share the same influences as Morocco but their cuisine is less refined, more rustic. As a result of the French occupation, the spicing in Algeria is more subtle than that of its neighbours. Tunisians, by contrast, are fond of highly spiced dishes and like to anoint their food with liberal applications of *harissa* – a fiery paste made of red chillies, garlic, cumin, coriander, dried mint and olive oil. At the same time, they enjoy a legacy of pasta and tomatoes, left by the Italian colonists. The food of Libya is the simplest in the region – a peasant diet akin to that eaten hundreds of years ago by the invading Arabs.

Egypt has more in common with Turkey, Greece and the Middle East than with its North African neighbours, and many of the dishes eaten regularly in Egypt have their origins elsewhere. The taste that homesick Egyptians are most likely to yearn for is *ful medames* – a purée made of small, dried broad beans, and enlivened with lemon juice, olive oil and garlic. Falafel is another distinctively Egyptian dish – little rissoles made of ground dried chickpeas or *ful* and spices. Bread is an indispensable part of the diet. Indeed it was the Egyptians who discovered how to make leavened bread several thousand years ago, and its importance is evident in the name for their most common bread, *aish*, derived from the word for 'life'.

Although the meaning of the name Mahgreb may be 'unfamiliar', this does not apply to its cuisine. Many of the flavours and ingredients once only available at speciality shops are now easily found on supermarket shelves. Whether you are looking for preserved lemons, green tea or couscous grains to create an authentic Mahgreb meal you need not search too far. Soon your kitchen will be brimming with the aromas and flavours of this area of North Africa.

ABOVE: **1** caraway **2** dried ginger **3** saffron threads
4 argan oil **5** cinnamon stick **6** ground cinnamon
7 pomegranate molasses **8** harissa

chicken and vegetables. In Tunisia it is made with rabbit or mutton and chickpeas, and served with a spicy, chilli-hot sauce. In Algeria the amount of meat may be minimal but there will be a wide variety of vegetables, such as broad beans, artichokes, aubergines, fennel, peas, courgettes and potatoes.

The art of making complex pastries may have been learned from the Turks but arguably the North African countries have refined it still further. In Morocco, the almost impossibly thin *ouarka* pastry is still made by hand, and used to produce a variety of delicate little pastries – plus the famous *b'stilla* or *pastilla*, where layer upon layer of crisp pastry is interleaved with pigeon, nuts, dried fruit and lemony scrambled eggs, then finished with a sprinkling of cinnamon and sugar.

pickling and preserving jars

The unforgiving heat of the bright sunny days in the Mahgreb and the fear of scarcity are the major factors leading to the prevalence of preserved foods. Before the common use of refrigeration, this was the only means by which cooks could make food last more than a few days. The preserved foods have become everyday ingredients now in the popular cooking of the area.

1 Glass jar with metal lid This sort of glass jar is suitable for preserving foods that will be left on show for all to admire. The ornate lid, while providing a neat fit, will probably not create a tight seal, so this jar might not be used for sweet pickles or jellies.

2 Glass jar with glass lid The glass lid on this jar is closed using a metal rim and lever to clip the lid down. There is usually also a rubber ring placed between the lid and the jar to form a tight seal enabling more liquid preserves, such as preserved lemons, to be kept.

3 Stoneware jar When the contents of the jar do not need to be seen, a jar such as this is fine. Small amounts of spice or herb pastes could be stored in these.

4 Ceramic jar This glazed ceramic jar is minimally decorated making it suitable to be used at the table and not just in the kitchen. Perhaps it might hold the *dukkah* to be used as a seasoning mixture on top of whatever food is being served.

preserved lemons

Cut 6 lemons into quarters, taking cuts to within 1cm of the base. Measure 350g coarse sea salt and pack some of this into the centre of each lemon, press to re-form to shape. Sterilise a 1 litre preserving jar and fill with half the remaining salt. Pack the lemons in tightly. Push in 3 bay leaves. Mix the remaining salt with 2 tbsp caster sugar, 15 allspice berries, 15 coriander seeds and 5 star anise; sprinkle over the lemons. Add the juice of 6 more lemons. Seal and store for 1 month, turning the jar daily. When using, cut off the flesh and use only the peel.

pigeon tagine with preserved lemon

If you've ever had the pleasure of tasting one of Morocco's greatest foods, the *tagine* or *tageen*, you will undoubtedly agree that the word stew is hardly adequate to describe it. There are endless varieties, some made with savoury spices, to those with sweeter flavours made with fresh and dried fruits. This is a pigeon and cauliflower version, which I tasted in a restaurant high in the Atlas Mountains – a very remote spot. The dish was cooked in a *touagen slaouis*, the conical shaped earthenware pot which holds the steam and prevents the food from drying our during lengthy cooking. A good casserole or heavy metal pan with a lid will suffice.

Serves 4
Preparation time: 1 hour 35 minutes

Ingredients
75g unsalted butter
4 x 550g squab pigeons, cut in half
1 onion, chopped
2 garlic cloves, crushed
1 tsp ground cinnamon
1 tsp ground ginger
½ tsp caraway seeds
good pinch of saffron or ½ tsp powdered, soaked in 60ml hot water
1 tsp sweet paprika
1 tsp turmeric
1 red chilli, chopped
salt and freshly ground black pepper
small bunch fresh coriander, tied with string
1 head cauliflower, cut into florets
2 red peppers, roasted, seeded, cut into wide ribbons
50g green olives
½ preserved lemon, pulp removed, cut into strips (see page 119)

Method
1 Melt the butter in a large casserole or pan, then when hot add the pigeon halves and fry until golden brown. Remove with a slotted spoon and set aside. Fry the onion and garlic in the same pan until golden, then add the spices, the chilli and a little salt and pepper.
2 Return the pigeon to the onions and garlic, add 600ml water, bring to the boil, tuck in the coriander and cover with a lid. Reduce the heat, simmer for 50 minutes or until the pigeons are very tender.
3 Remove the pigeon halves with a slotted spoon and set aside. Discard the coriander. Add the cauliflower florets and simmer on the stove until just cooked, remove and keep warm.
4 Return the pigeon to the sauce, add the roasted pepper strips and cauliflower florets, return to the boil.
5 Arrange the pigeons on a large serving dish, pile the vegetables in a mound on top. Scatter with the olives and strips of preserved lemon rind. Serve immediately with Moroccan bread to mop up the sauce.

Tools
Large casserole
Slotted spoon

pastry tools

Many people avoid working with pastry thinking that it requires great skill to create the perfect tart, flan etc. In fact all that needs to be remembered is that pastry should just be handled gently and as little as possible. In most instances it is best to make the pastry ahead of time and leave it in the refrigerator for an hour, since it is easiest to work with when cold. The tools used with pastry in the countries of the Mahgreb are similar to those in the West and perform the same functions. Make sure you have enough space on the work top or table before you start.

1, 2 Pastry cutters These round cutters are often bought in sets of rings progressing from about 2–7.5cm across. They are made of tin and can have either fluted or plain edges giving a slightly different finish.

3 Rolling pin Although this wooden rolling pin is a lot thinner and longer than most found in our kitchens, it works in just the same way. These are made longer so that they can be used to roll out very wide sheets of pastry.

4 Pastry brushes Brushes come in various sizes – suitable for large or small areas. The handles are made of wood and the bristles are either plastic or natural bristle. They have many uses from coating pastry, to greasing tins and dusting with flour

Technique for rolling and cutting pastry

It is almost always important to use pastry that is well chilled. Before you start working with the pastry you must make sure the work surface is completely clean and free from debris or this will become rolled into the pastry. Dust the surface well with flour and start rolling the pastry gently. To start with turn the pastry 90° after each roll in order to create an even round shape. As the pastry gets wider give it a few rolls before each turn, handling the pastry very carefully and keeping the work surface and rolling pin well floured to stop sticking. Once you have the correct thickness, either use small cutters to create the shapes you need or use the whole sheet to line the tin that you intend to use.

5 Baking beans Traditionally when tarts or pastry shells are baked blind, they are lined with parchment paper and then filled with beans to stop the pastry from rising during the cooking. You can use dried beans or these clay versions which are the same size and shape as natural beans but last for ever.

Tools

Shallow dish
Bowl
2 saucepans
Slotted spoon
Teacloth
Frying pan
Tagine or 23cm pie tin
Brush

Ingredients

250g monkfish fillet,
    skinless, cut into 5cm
    lengths
150g sea bass fillet,
    skinless, cut into 5cm
    lengths
150g small Norwegian
    prawns, peeled
200g large Tiger prawns,
    peeled
2 tsp salt
80g garlic cloves,
    crushed
1 large bunch fresh
    coriander, chopped
100ml white wine
    vinegar
100ml lemon juice
½ tsp cayenne
1 tbsp paprika
1 tsp fresh saffron
2 tsp ground cumin
1kg spinach, stems
    removed
100ml virgin olive oil
150g unsalted butter
2kg tomatoes, skinned,
    seeded, chopped
12 sheets filo pastry
1 egg, beaten
chopped parsley, paprika
    and lemon shreds,
    to garnish

Method

1 Wash the fish and prawns and place in a shallow dish with the salt for 1 minute; remove, rinse off the salt and pat the fish and prawns dry. Place the garlic and coriander in a bowl, add the vinegar, lemon juice and cayenne. Add the paprika, saffron and cumin. Add the fish, leaving to marinate for 1 hour. Preheat the oven to 160°C/Gas 3.

2 Blanch the spinach in boiling salted water for 30 seconds, then remove with a slotted spoon into iced water to refresh. Drain and dry in a teacloth.

3 Remove the fish from the marinade and reserve the marinade.

4 Heat the oil and 100g of the butter in a frying pan, add the fish fillets and prawns and cook for 2–3 minutes on each side until golden.

5 Mix half the reserved marinade with the cooked spinach and the other half with the chopped tomatoes. In separate pans, cook the tomatoes and the spinach until dry.

6 To assemble the *pastilla*, using 6 sheets of filo, and buttering the top of them as you work, lay each one across the base of the *tagine* at a different angle, so that they cover the base completely and overhang the edge (1).

7 Spread the spinach evenly over the filo base, then top with the tomatoes. Lay the fish on top, then pull the overhanging pastry to the centre (2).

8 Lay the remaining 6 sheets of filo on a work surface, buttering and overlapping them as before. Cut out a rough circle about 25cm across and lay it on top of the fish. Tuck the edges around the bottom layer like a bed sheet (3).

9 Brush the top with more butter and the beaten egg wash. Place in the oven to bake for 30 minutes until crisp and golden. Use kitchen paper to blot any excess oil, then serve immediately. Boujemma Mars garnishes the *pastilla* with chopped parsley, paprika and lemon shreds.

1

2

3

seafood pastilla
pastilla aux fruits de mer

Pastilla (French) or *B'Stilla* (Moroccan) are small pies made of a gossamer-like dough called *ouarka*, very similar to Greek *filo*, which is now often used in its place as *ouarka* is difficult and time consuming to make. The seafood *pastilla* is a recent addition to the Moroccan culinary repertoire: it reflects the modern trends for lighter dishes. This particular recipe is from chef boujemma mars, chef at Morocco's renowned Mamounia Hotel in Marrakech. Boujemma is a great exponent of creating modern Moroccan dishes while not loosing sight of tradition.

Serves 6–8
Preparation Time: 1 hour 50 minutes including marinating

chopping nuts

Whole nuts are one of the worlds greatest snack foods, but for cooking they really do need chopping up, not only to decrease their size but also to release their flavours into the recipes. The level of fineness or coarseness depends on your own taste and their function within the recipe. For example, almonds that are chopped extremely fine or almost ground can be used in place of flour for baking, while sliced almonds provide crunchy addition to salads. The tools you choose for chopping nuts depend on what is available and for what the nuts are to be used.

1 Mortar and pestle These can be made from a variety of materials, but the most common is this ceramic version. Both the mortar (bowl) and pestle end (crusher) are made from unglazed ceramic, while the pestle handle is made of wood. The nuts are placed in the mortar and then the pestle is initially used to break them up from above with a few sharp blows. The pestle is then moved around the mortar in a stirring action to crush the nuts to the required level.

2 Rolling pin The rolling pin makes a handy tool to crush nuts. The easiest method is to place the nuts in a sealed plastic bag, then carefully but firmly roll the pin over them. Occasionally shake the nuts back into a pile and continue to roll over them until they are finely crushed.

3 Knife This is the classic way to chop nuts. The larger the knife the easier and quicker the job will be, but do not choose a knife too unwieldy to handle. Hold the point of the knife down with one hand while you move the handle up and down with the other.

4 Nut crackers The traditional hinged nut cracker is invaluable if you have nuts that are still in their shells. Place the nut between either the larger or smaller area of the end nearest to the hinge and squeeze the two handles together just until the shell cracks. At this point you can remove most of the shell by hand and give it another crack is there is any more shell to be removed. Be careful not crush the nuts too hard if you wish to get the shell off neatly.

egyptian vegetable salad with dukkah

Unlike many European style salads, Mediterranean salads are more than just lettuce and cucumber. Raw and cooked vegetables are often prepared together, usually seasoned with spices. The variations are endless. *Dukkah* is a spiced seasoning of mixed nuts and seeds, very popular in Egypt, and is served in dishes throughout the day – breakfast, snacks and *mezze*.

Serves 4
Preparation Time: 20 minutes

Ingredients

1 red pepper, seeded, cut into thick ribbons
4 medium tomatoes
300g cooked white haricot beans
1 red onion, thinly sliced
12 black olives
2 hard-boiled eggs, quartered
1 tbsp chopped fresh coriander
3 tbsp olive oil
1 tbsp white wine vinegar

For the *dukkah*

50g blanched whole almonds or hazelnuts
40g sesame seeds
25g coriander seeds
5g cumin seeds
½ tsp coarse sea salt
¼ tsp cracked black pepper

Tools

Small frying pan
Mortar and pestle or small blender
Bowl

Method

1 First prepare the *dukkah*: heat a dry frying pan and when hot, throw in the almonds and seeds, stirring them all the time, and toast for 30 seconds. Place in a mortar and crush. Add the salt and pepper and crush with the pestle, not too fine.
2 Place all the salad ingredients in a bowl and toss gently together.
3 Arrange on a serving dish, sprinkle 1 tbsp of the prepared *dukkah* over and serve.

chopping herbs

A sprinkling of fresh herbs is often the finishing touch to a recipe, but herbs can also form the backbone of a dish such as a salad, or herb-filled rice pilaf. In these cases the dried herbs in glass jars just will not do. The vibrant colour and flavour from fresh leaves are essential. In some cases the leaves can be simply torn or added whole but for most recipes, the herbs are at their best when freshly chopped. If you feel uncomfortable handling a large knife or do not have the time, there are a variety of electrical or mechanised tools at your disposal.

1

2

1 Mini blender This electric blender performs a multitude of functions, one of them being the chopping of herbs. The leaves are placed in the container at the bottom with a two-armed blade. Once the top is secure the machine can be turned on and within seconds the herbs are finely chopped.

2 Push down herb chopper Like the electric version, the herbs are placed in the container at the bottom, but the blades are attached to the top part. Once the handle and blade mechanism is attached you press down on the handle which chops the herbs and rotates the blades between each chop.

3 Mini herb mill This little gadget is a mill with a hinged lid which can be opened: a blade is fitted and a small amount of herbs placed inside the mill. The mill is then closed and the herbs are chopped by pulling the cord, which makes the blade whiz round.

4 Makrata A very sharp straight blade is riveted to a wooden handle to form this effective tool. Large amounts of herbs can be chopped on a board using this. As the herbs spread out, they can be brought back into a pile with a sweeping action of the blade across the board. The herbs are chopped with an up and down motion of the blade through the leaves.

3

4

5 Hachoir This chopping knife is in a half-moon shape with a wooden handle at one side. It is used in a bowl, usually made of wood, that is shaped in just the same way as the blade. Small amounts of herbs are placed in the bowl and chopped using a rocking action of the blade back and forth to the desired fineness.

5

north african pasta

Food historians have long been of the opinion that pasta was invented in the Middle East. It was then taken to China by traders, and returned to its supposed Italian homeland through the travels of Marco Polo. Today pasta is used extensively in the Mahgreb – considered a quick and healthy family food as elsewhere in the world. Argan oil is extracted from the nut of the fruit of the Argan tree, grown all over North Africa. The nuts are pressed like olives, extracting the delicate oil, highly prized by connoisseurs. If you can not get argan oil, use all olive oil instead.

Serves 4
Preparation Time: 15 minutes

Tools
Large pan
Pasta tongs
Small blender

Ingredients
500g thin noodle pasta
   (spaghetti or linguine)
salt and freshly ground
   black pepper
4 tbsp virgin olive oil
2 garlic cloves, crushed
4 tbsp chopped fresh
   flat-leaf parsley
100g whole blanched
   almonds, roasted
2 tbsp argan oil
cayenne
40g Parmesan cheese
   shavings

Method
1 Cook the pasta in a large pan of boiling salted water until *al dente*, drain reserving 100ml of the cooking liquid. Season the pasta lightly then add 1 tbsp of the olive oil. Dress in a serving dish.
2 In a small blender, whiz together the garlic, parsley and almonds to a coarse purée. While the motor is running, drizzle both the oils and the reserved cooking liquid into the garlic mixture, and season to taste with salt, pepper and cayenne.
3 To serve, pour the dressing over the pasta, sprinkle the Parmesan shavings over and serve immediately.

roast chicken with hot green chillies

Harissa (or *hereesa*) is a fiery hot chilli and garlic paste used extensively in the Mahgreb, but mainly in Tunisia, usually served with Tunisian couscous. Traditionally, it is made with hot red chillies, but here I replace them with fresh green chillies and use the mix to spread under the skin of the chicken, to add an extra flavour to the bird. You can buy red *harissa* in Middle Eastern stores either in tubes or cans, and it will work equally well in this dish.

Serves 4
Preparation Time: 1 hour 25 minutes

Tools	Ingredients	Method
Small blender Roasting pan with rack	¼ large bunch coriander stalks (from the chopped coriander used in the *harissa*) 1 x 1.5kg free range chicken 3 tbsp virgin olive oil 50g unsalted butter, softened **For the green *harissa* paste** 6 long green chillies, seeded, finely chopped 2 garlic cloves, crushed 4 tbsp chopped fresh coriander 1 tsp ground cumin 1 tsp dried mint 1 tsp ground coriander 5 tbsp virgin olive oil salt	**1** Preheat the oven to 200°C/Gas 6. For the *harissa*, place all the ingredients in a small blender, except for the oil and salt. Whiz to a smooth paste, then add enough oil to form a paste, season with a little salt. **2** Place the coriander stalks in the body cavity of the chicken. **3** Using your fingers, gently separate the chicken skin from the breast meat and spread the *harissa* paste evenly under the skin, covering as much of the flesh as possible. Rub any remaining paste over the legs and outside of the chicken. **4** Place the chicken on a rack in a roasting pan, drizzle the olive oil over and rub the butter over. Place in the oven for 1–1½ hours or until cooked and the juices run clear when the leg is pierced with a sharp knife. **5** Serve the whole chicken on a serving dish, or cut into pieces if preferred, with the pan juices poured over and accompanied by steamed couscous. This dish is also excellent using quails instead of chicken, use 2 quails for each serving.

moroccan earthenware pots

Despite the complex and exotic nature of much Moroccan cooking, the utensils used are very simple. Many households have little more than an assortment of hand-made, glazed earthenware pots, and it is quite usual not to possess an oven. Instead, the pots are placed over the hearth and sometimes left overnight in the glowing embers to simmer away slowly.

Earthenware is a good-natured cooking material that retains heat well and keeps in all the moisture, so it is ideal for slow-cooked dishes. Do bear in mind, though, that it doesn't cope well with sudden changes of temperature.

1 Magmar This burner is typical of the kind found in Moroccan homes. It is filled with charcoal and set underneath a tagine for cooking stews.

2 Kadra This pot is traditionally used for cooking pulses such as split peas and lentils. The tight-fitting, dome-shaped lid ensures that all the moisture is retained.

3 Tangiya The *tangiya* is used to bake lamb and spices in a charcoal oven. The narrow neck minimises moisture loss, and the handles make it easy to carry.

4 Tagra The *tagra* is ideal for cooking whole fish or large fish steaks on a bed of spiced vegetables – and in a minimum of liquid to preserve the wonderful flavours.

5 Tagine slaouis The classic tagine is used to cook the stew of the same name. It is topped with a tall, conical lid designed to keep in all the steam and prevent food from drying out.

6 Tabsel The *tabsel* has many uses in Moroccan cooking. A typical recipe is meatballs in tomato sauce with eggs broken into the centre and cooked until just set.

tagine of lamb with prunes and honey

This recipe, typical of Morocco's legendary sweet tagines, comes from joyce goldstein, one of the world's great cookery writers. Joyce's books have made her a legend amongs food lovers and this recipe is a culinary triumph. Serve it with a good steaming bowl of couscous.

Serves 6–8
Preparation Time: 1 hour 20 minutes

Ingredients
450g pitted prunes
4 tbsp olive oil or vegetable oil
50g unsalted butter
2kg boneless lamb shoulder, trimmed well, cut into 4cm cubes
2 medium onions, chopped

2 tsp ground coriander
1½ tsp ground ginger
pinch of saffron
600ml lamb stock or water
5 tbsp honey
salt and freshly ground black pepper
2 tbsp sesame seeds, toasted

Tools

Bowl
Large frying pan
Large casserole
Slotted spoon
Tagine and charcoal burner

Method

1 Soak the prunes in a bowl of warm water until needed. Heat 2 tbsp of the oil and 2 tbsp of the butter in a heavy frying pan over a high heat. Add as many lamb cubes as will fit without crowding and brown on all sides. Transfer to a large casserole. Repeat with the remaining lamb, adding a little more oil and butter.

2 Heat the remaining oil and butter in the same pan over a high heat, add the onions, cook until translucent, about 10 minutes. Add the spices, cook for 3 minutes. Transfer the onion mixture to the casserole with the lamb, add enough stock or water to barely cover the meat.

3 Bring to the boil, reduce the heat and simmer, uncovered, for about 45 minutes. Drain the prunes and add to the stew; continue cooking until the lamb is very tender, about 20 minutes more.

4 Add the honey, and salt and pepper to taste. Transfer to a tagine for serving, sprinkle with the sesame seeds, and serve with couscous.

dersa chicken tagine with egg pancake
djaj souiri

The North African countries are especially fond of serving eggs with meat dishes, perhaps as a way of adding richness to a dish. This tagine of chicken is highly spiced with *dersa*, pounded chilli and garlic, added to meat dishes, a cousin of the local *harissa*. The tagine is finished in the oven, cooked under a thin egg pancake that makes for an unusual presentation. This dish comes from Essaouira, a town along Morocco's Atlantic coast.

Serves 4
Preparation Time: 45 minutes

Method

1 Heat an ovenproof casserole with the oil and butter. Season the chicken pieces with and fry until golden and just cooked, about 20–25 minutes. Remove with a slotted spoon.

2 Return the casserole to the heat, add the onion and fry until golden; add 400ml water, simmer for 10 minutes. Return the chicken to the casserole and add the cooked chickpeas and their liquid. Preheat the oven to 180°C/Gas 4.

3 Blend all the ingredients for the *dersa* with a little water in a small blender to form a thick paste, then stir into the chicken joints and cook for a further 10 minutes.

4 In a bowl, whisk together the eggs with the cumin, paprika and saffron and 100ml water. Pour the egg mix over the chicken, then place in the oven to bake, uncovered, until the egg pancake is cooked, about 3–4 minutes.

5 Sprinkle the coriander over and serve from the oven with lots of bread.

Ingredients

3 tbsp vegetable oil
500g unsalted butter
1 x 1.5kg free-range
  chicken, cut into
  8 small joints
salt and freshly ground
  black pepper
1 onion, chopped
200g canned cooked
  chickpeas
2 tbsp chopped fresh
  coriander, to serve

For the *dersa*
4 garlic cloves, chopped
1 hot red chilli, seeded
salt and freshly ground
  black pepper
pinch of sweet paprika

For the pancakes
4 eggs
1 tsp ground cumin
½ tsp sweet paprika
⅛ tsp powdered saffron

Tools
Ovenproof casserole
Slotted spoon
Small blender
Wooden spoon
Bowl
Whisk

stewed broad beans egyptian style
ful medames

These tiny broad beans are native to Egypt and the Levant. Known as the national dish of Egypt, *ful medames* is a breakfast dish of slow cooked beans prepared in special pot called a *idra* or *dammasa*, with a narrow neck so that the minimal amount of water is required. During my many years in hotels, I have lost count of the times I've cooked and served this dish to Middle Eastern and European guests alike. It may be served on its own, but it is usual to serve a selection of chopped garnish to offer alongside.

Serves 4–6
Preparation Time: 3 hours 25 minutes plus overnight soaking

Ingredients
450g dried broad beans
  (*ful*), soaked overnight
  with several changes
  of water
150g red lentils
2 garlic cloves, crushed
1 tsp ground cumin
salt
100ml virgin olive oil

To serve
2 hard boiled eggs,
  chopped
2 tomatoes, chopped
1 red onion, finely sliced
2 tbsp chopped fresh
  flat-leaf parsley
lemon wedges

Tools
Large pan
Blender

Method
1 Place the soaked beans in an large pan, cover with 1 litre water, bring to the boil. Add the lentils, cover with a lid, cook for 3 hours or until tender, adding more water if necessary during the cooking time.
2 Add the garlic, along with the cumin, cook for a further 10 minutes, finally add salt to taste.
3 Process about one quarter of the mixture to a purée, return to the pan and stir to mix.
4 To serve, divide the beans between 4 soup plates or bowls, drizzle the olive oil over and serve with a selection of garnishes.

Note
The cooked beans may be puréed in a blender, drizzled with olive oil and served as a hearty soup with the garnishes alongside.

steaming

Steaming is the ideal way to get the best flavour out of food without adding anything in the way of fat. You are also preventing the flavours and nutrients leaching out into boiling water. The food is placed in a perforated container above the simmering water or stew. As the steam rises from the liquid below it cooks the food. You can buy steamer pans that come with a steamer insert that sits over the base pan with a tight-fitting lid. You can also use fold-out steamers that sit in the base of a saucepan and hold the food above the water. Almost any food can be steamed from vegetables to whole sweet or savoury puddings.

1 Couscousière or *keskes* A couscousière is a tall, double pot used for cooking couscous. The stew, which can be made with meat, fish or vegetables, is cooked in the bottom of the pot, while the couscous is placed in a perforated steamer that fits on top and is covered with a tight-fitting lid. In this way, the couscous absorbs the flavour from the stew. Traditional couscousières are made of unglazed earthenware but they are now readily available in metal.

---

seven vegetable couscous with dried fruits and ras el hanout

This is my modern Moroccan vegetarian version of its national dish. Every Moroccan housewife has her own treasured recipe for couscous on which she spends hours of preparation. I have used quick couscous which works well if you take care and the spice mix *ras el hanout* is available from specialist spice or north African stores. Why seven vegetables and not six? Traditionally in Morocco seven is a lucky number, and this dish is served usually on a Friday evening, and always as part of a Moroccan feast or *diffa*, just to ensure no one leaves hungry!

Serves 4–6
Preparation Time: 1 hour 50 minutes plus overnight soaking

Ingredients

150g dried chickpeas, soaked
  overnight
3 litres vegetable stock or water
3 garlic cloves, crushed
½ tsp tumeric
½ tsp saffron or powdered saffron
¼ tsp cinnamon
90g unsalted butter

4 tbsp olive oil
1 tbsp *ras el hanout*
400g tomatoes, skinned, chopped
2 large parsnips, cut into wedges
400g pumpkin, cut into large cubes
2 large turnips, cut into wedges
3 carrots, cut into 2.5cm slices
4 baby courgettes, cut into
  2.5cm slices

2 onions cut into wedges
1 swede, cut into large cubes
75g raisins
75g dried dates
100g dried apricots
500g quick cook couscous
1 large bunch fresh coriander,
  chopped

Method

1 In a large pan, place the soaked chickpeas, vegetable stock, garlic, dried spices and butter and cook for 1½ hours or until tender. Drain the chickpeas and strain off the liquid.

2 In the base of a couscousière (or the base of a steamer with a tight fitting lid), heat the olive oil; when warm, add the *ras el hanout* to infuse for 30 seconds, then pour in the chickpea stock.

3 Add the tomatoes, vegetables and dried fruits and simmer for 15 minutes.

4 Steam the quick couscous, according to instructions on the packet, in the top of the couscousière or in a colander over the vegetables, about 15 minutes (if using a colander, you may have to line it with cheesecloth if holes are too big).

5 After 30 minutes in total, the vegetables are ready. Add the chopped coriander and the chickpeas to the vegetables and reheat for a couple of minutes.

6 Pile the hot couscous in a mound in the centre of a large serving dish, arrange the vegetables and fruits around the couscous and pour the remaining broth over and serve. In Tunisia it is customary to serve *harissa* as an accompaniment, not so in Morocco.

Tools

Large saucepan
Couscousière or
  saucepan /steamer
  with tight fitting lid;
  colander

water bottles

Water is a vital element and cooking ingredient in the countries of the Mahgreb. With the hot dry climate that they experience, water takes on a new importance, whether it is for drinking, cooking with or as nourishment for the growing crops. As well as straight water, there is also a great use of delicately flavoured waters. These are highly prized and used sparingly. You can often see water sellers on the souks with great flasks on their backs, portioning out small amounts to sell for a refreshing drink.

1,2,3 Water bottles These highly decorated bottles are used to contain the various different types of flavoured waters. These one are from Morocco, but similar bottles will be found throughout the Mahgreb. The waters are flavoured with additions such as rose petals, orange blossoms and gum Arabic. The water is distilled with the flavouring ingredients to create a very pure flavoured liquid. The waters can be diluted and used as drinks, but also within recipes such as the *basboussa* (below) or sprinkled over salads or in stews. They are also sometimes used to create a pleasant aroma in rooms by scattering a few drops around. In the West similar flavoured waters can now easily be bought in most supermarkets and delicatessens.

semolina and almond cake
basboussa

This moist almond flavoured semolina cake is made throughout the Middle East and the Mahgreb, albeit under different names. The cake, when baked, is coated with a syrup made with orange-flavour water while still hot.

Makes 12 squares
Preparation Time: 55 minutes

Method

1 Preheat the oven to 180°C/Gas 4. Make a light syrup by dissolving the sugar in a pan with the lemon juice and water, simmer until the syrup thickens, about 10 minutes, then add the orange-flavour water. Remove from the heat, keep warm.

2 Melt the butter in a pan. Pour into a large bowl, mix in the remaining ingredients, stir well together, spoon into a shallow 20–25cm baking tray.

3 Bake for 30 minutes until golden, remove from the oven and cool slightly before cutting with a sharp knife into rectangles or diamonds while still in the tray.

4 Pour the syrup over, return to the oven and bake for a further 5 minutes. Serve warm or at room temperature.

Tools

2 small pans
1 large bowl
20–25cm baking tray

Ingredients

100g unsalted butter
125g fine semolina
150g caster sugar
100g ground almonds
50g plain flour
50ml full fat milk
1 tsp baking soda
½ tsp vanilla essence
12 blanched whole
    almonds

For the syrup

100g caster sugar
½ tbsp lemon juice
75ml boiling water
2 tbsp orange-flavour
    water

coffee and tea

Because the predominant religion of the region, Islam, forbids the consumption of alcohol, much more is made of the other drinks available such as coffee and tea. The rituals involved in the making of these drinks form an important part of the whole drinking experience. The coffee is served very strong, dark and often sweet in small amounts. Tea is extremely popular, being served in Morocco before and after most meals, as well as being sipped for hours well into the night in many cafés. The tea is mostly green or made from herbs and usually sweet.

1 Coffee pots These long-handled metal pots are placed directly over the heat. The finely ground coffee is combined with sugar and water and heated until the mixture begins to rise in the pot. It is then stirred, returned to the heat for a moment and poured straight into small cups.

2 Tea pot Tea is often made in a pot such as this. The water is in the bottom while the tea is placed in the top part which has tiny perforations at its base. As the water below comes to a boil, it rises and saturates the leaves above. It then falls back into the pot.

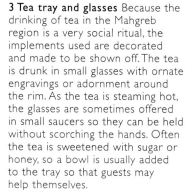

3 Tea tray and glasses Because the drinking of tea in the Mahgreb region is a very social ritual, the implements used are decorated and made to be shown off. The tea is drunk in small glasses with ornate engravings or adornment around the rim. As the tea is steaming hot, the glasses are sometimes offered in small saucers so they can be held without scorching the hands. Often the tea is sweetened with sugar or honey, so a bowl is usually added to the tray so that guests may help themselves.

suppliers

The following list includes sources of the ingredients and equipment featured in the photographs in this book, as well as other useful suppliers and producers of fine foods.

CENTRAL MEDITERRANEAN

Brindisa
32 Exmouth Market
London EC1R 3LU
Tel: 020 7713 1666
Web: www.brindisa.com
Hard-to-find Spanish foods, including beans, canned fish and meats.

Camisa & Son
61 Old Compton Street
London W1D 6AS
Tel: 020 7437 7610
Superb Italian deli selling authentic pasta, oils and dried mushrooms.

Carluccio's
28A Neal Street
London WC2 9PS
Tel: 020 7240 1487
Web: www.carluccios.com
Impressive range of quality Italian foods, including own-brand pasta.

Mr Christian's
11 Elgin Crescent
London W11 2JA
Tel: 020 7229 0501
International deli selling fresh pasta, ethnic breads, olives, oils and dry goods.

Continental Chef Supplies
The Courtyard
South Hetton Industrial Estate
County Durham
DH6 2UZ
Tel: 0808 1001 777
Web: www.chef.net
Kitchen equipment mainly for the hotel and restaurant trade.

P De La Fuente
288 Portobello Road
London W10 5TE
Tel: 020 8960 5687
Spanish delicatessen.

Divertimenti
33–34 Marylebone High Street
London W1U 4PT
Tel: 020 7935 0689
Web: www.divertimenti.co.uk
Italian pasta machines, pizza stones and hand-painted pottery, Spanish griddles, French porcelain ovenware. Good selection of oils and dried herbs.

La Fromagerie
2–4 Moxon Street
London W1
Tel: 020 7935 0341, and
30 Highbury Park
London N5 2AA
Tel: 020 7359 7440
Web: www.lafromagerie.co.uk
Superb cheeses (matured on the premises), as well as other fine foods, including olives and pasta.

R Garcia & Sons
248–250 Portobello Road
London W11 1LL
Tel: 020 7221 6119
Everything Spanish from the traditional cazuelas to paella pans of every size. Good selection of Spanish olives, oils, ham and cheeses.

The Gazzano's Ltd
167-169 Farringdon Road
London EC1R 3AL
Tel: 020 7 250 1002
All Italian foods, both fresh and packaged.

Harrods Food Hall
87–135 Brompton Road
Knightsbridge
London SW1X 7XL
Tel: 020 7730 1234
Web: www.harrods.com
Splendid charcuterie, cheeses, deli items, dried fruits and nuts.

Harvey Nichols Food Hall
109–125 Knightsbridge
London SW1X 7RJ
Tel: 020 7235 5000
Web: www.harveynichols.com
Lush emporium of excellent foods of all kinds – beautifully packaged.

Lina Stores
18 Brewer Street
London W1R 3FS
Tel: 020 7437 6482
Italian delicatessen specialising in fresh pasta.

Luigi's
349 Fulham Road
London SW10 9TW
Tel: 020 7352 7739
Wide range of Italian food including fresh pasta and groceries

Lupe Pinto's Deli
24 Leven Street
Edinburgh EH3 9LJ
Tel: 0131 228 6241
Web: www.lupepintos.com
Specialist deli stocking Spanish foods. Also in Glasgow.

David Mellor
4 Sloane Square
London SW1W 8EE
Tel: 020 7730 4259
Web: ww.davidmellordesign.co.uk
Traditional British/French kitchen shop. Selection of knives, solid wood boards, whisks of every kind, white china, pottery and glassware.

Oliviers & Co.
114 Ebury Street
London SW1W 9QD
Tel: 020 7823 6770
Web: www.oliviers-co.com
Olive oils and specialities from around the Mediterranean.

Rias Altas Delicatessen
97 Frampton Street
London NW8 8NA
Tel: 020 7262 4340
Spanish deli with a good range of hams, preserves, olives and pulses.

Selfridges Food Hall
400 Oxford Street
London W1A 1AB
Tel: 08708 377 377
Web: www.selfridges.com
A wide range of fine foods.

Speck Delicatessen
2 Holland Park Terrace
Portland Road
London W11 4ND
Tel: 020 7229 7005
Excellent Italian deli products, condiments and salamis.

The Spice Shop
1 Blenheim Crescent
London W11 2EE
Tel: 020 7221 4448. Web: www.thespiceshoponline.com
Additive-free herbs and spices, and also oddities such as tapioca.

Valvona & Crolla
19 Elm Row
Edinburgh EH7
Tel: 0131 556 6066
Web: www.valvonacrolla.com
Famous, exuberant and authentic Italian deli with huge range of high-quality produce.

Villandry
170 Great Portland Street,
London W1
Tel: 020 7631 3131
High-class deli foods, cheeses, wines and dry goods.

BALKANS

T Adamou & Sons
124–126 Chiswick High Road
London W4 1PU
Tel: 020 8994 0752
Old established Greek-Cypriot food store with fresh vegetables, groceries, olive oils, bread, cheeses all from the Mediterranean area, including some Arabic specialities and Turkish coffee pots.

Archie Foodstore
14 Moscow Road
London W2 4BT
Tel: 020 7229 2275
Small but excellent stock of Greek, Turkish and Middle Eastern foods, including pulses, nuts and syrups.

Athenian Grocery
16A Moscow Road
London W2 7AX
Tel: 020 7229 6280
Greek Cypriot and continental store with fresh produce from Cyprus every morning.

Yasar Halim
493–495 Green Lanes
London N4 1AL
Tel: 0208 340 8090
Turkish shop selling a large range of sweet and savoury pastries in their bakery, as well as imported vegetables and spices.

Iman Food Store
77 Abbey Road
London NW8 0AE
Tel: 020 7372 1100
Iranian store stocking produce and groceries from many of the Mediterranean countries, including unusual fruit. Good bakery section.s.

Andreas Michli
33 Salisbury Road
Haringey
London N4 1JY
Tel: 0208 802 0188
A Greek treasure trove filled with seasonal produce from Cyprus and from his own organic farm in Hertfordshire along with olives, vine leaves, Greek oils and all manner of traditional terracotta pots, saucepans and baking trays.

Sama Foods
578–580 Green Lanes
London N8 0RP
Tel: 020 8211 7681
A large warehouse open to the public, selling every kind of Turkish cookware: Tavas trays, casserole pots, modern and traditional. A range of olives, spices, Turkish coffee, biscuits and Turkish Delight.

Turkish Food Centre
89 Ridley Road
London E8 2NP
Tel: 020 7254 6754
The original shop of what is now a chain of 9 stores throughout the London region. Suppliers of Turkish groceries, fresh food and bakery goods, and food from the Mediterranean area.

Turkish Food Centre
227–229 Lewisham High Street
London SE13 6LY
Tel: 020 8318 0436
One of the branches of the shop listed above. Also has stores in Croydon, Catford and Edmonton among others.

EASTERN MEDITERRANEAN

Damasgate
81–85 Uxbridge Road
London W12 7NR
Tel: 020 8743 5116
Shop specialising in Syrian and Lebanese groceries and fresh produce. Also stocks Turkish, Greek and Arab foods.

Green Valley
36 Upper Berkeley Street
London W1H 7PG
Tel: 020 7402 7385
A deli-supermarket stocking everything from the Mediterranean and Middle Eastern region; nougats, preserved fruits from the Lebanon; a huge range of patisserie; Halal butchery; Arabic bread. Also has a catering service.

The Lebanese Food Centre
153–155 The Vale
Acton
London W3 7RH
Tel: 020 8740 7365
A retail outlet, owned by Mr Allouji, of Arconi Fine Foods, the wholesale company which supplies London with some of the finest Lebanese ingredients and produce.

SUPPLIERS CONTINUED

Nut Case Ltd.
352 Uxbridge Road
Shepherds Bush
London W12 7LL
Tel: 020 88743 0336
*Award-winning shop selling a
fantastic selection of nuts,
Lebanese sweets and Eastern
delights which you can sample
before you buy. Also sells a range
of brass coffee pots and coffee
beans.*

Panzer's
13–19 Circus Road
St John's Wood
London NW8 6PB
Tel: 020 7722 8596
Web: www.panzers.co.uk
*Superb Jewish deli items, dry
goods, and huge green grocery.*

Reza Patisserie
345 Kensington High Street
London W8 6NW
Tel: 020 7602 3674
*Turkish-Iranian deli, stock includes
patisserie, preserves, nuts, Iranian
caviar, Turkish sausages, dried fruit,
saffron and fresh herbs.*

Super Bahar
349A Kensington High Street
London W8 6NW
Tel: 020 7603 5083
*Iranian deli stocking nuts, desserts,
caviar and vegetables.*

MAHGREB AND EGYPT

Algerian Coffee Stores
52 Old Compton Street,
London W1V 6PB
Tel: 020 7437 2480
Web: www.algcoffee.co.uk
*Wonderful shop with around 100
different coffees and 140 teas.*

Fez
71 Goldborne Road
London W10 5NP
Tel: 020 8964 5573
*Traditional tagines, casseroles.
Moroccan trays, tea and coffee
pots, plus Moroccan soft
furnishings and lights.*

Le Maroc
94 Goldborne Road
London W10 5PS
Tel: 020 8968 9783
*Moroccan shop selling North
African groceries, olives, herbs, and
also tagine cooking pots.*

La Marrakech
64 Goldborne Road
London W10 5PS
Tel: 020 8964 8307
*Moroccan outlet with range of
olives, preserved lemons, herbs,
spices, olive oils, couscous and
fresh meat. Also stocks the
traditional Moroccan tea pots, tea
glasses, tagines and coucousières.*

bibliography

Boulud, Daniel, *Café Boulud Cookbook* (Scribner, 1999)

Demetriou, Polycarpos, *Food from the Village* (Thanos Press, 1998)

English, Todd, *The Olives Table* (Simon and Schuster, 1997)

Goldstein, Joyce, *Back to Square One* (Morrow, 1992)

Grigson, Sophie, *Sunshine Food* (BBC Books, 2000)

Guillon, Jean Claude, *The New Provençal Cooking* (Chronicle Books, 1995)

Helou, Anissa, *Lebanese Cuisine* (Grub Street, 1994)

Malouf, Greg, *Arabesque* (HGB, 1999)

Ozer, Huseyin, *Sofra Cookbook* (Thorsons, 1998)

Roden, Claudia, *Mediterranean Cookery* (BBC Books, 1987)

Sevilla, Mariá José, *Mediterranean Flavours* (Pavilion, 1995)

Vergé, Roger, *Entertaining with Roger Vergé* (Stewart, Tabori and Chang, 1986)

Wolfert, Paula, *Mediterranean Cooking* (Black Dog and Leventhal, 1996)

acknowledgements

AUTHOR: No book is the sole work of one person, and this book is no exception. There are so many people to thank for their support and friendship during the writing of it.

To my wife Anita and my family for their continual support with my writing.

To Jacqui Small for giving me the opportunity to write on such a fascinating and enjoyable subject – the Mediterranean. To Vicki Vrint and all the editorial team for their help and patience when occasional deadlines failed to be met. To Madeline Weston for her superb editing and great sense of humour at all times. To Linda Tubby and David Munns for their superb interpretation of my dishes in the photography; Penny Markam for her superb props; Jane Middleton, Anna Brandenburger whose writing skills have helped make this book a pleasure to do – I can't thank them enough. And Lara King who typed the manuscript. To my fellow contributors, chefs and authors who kindly consented to part with their wonderful recipes to make this book so special. To my good friend, Paul Goodfellow, managing director of Continental Chef Supplies, for kindly supplying the equipment for the Central Mediterranean chapter. To Fiona, Linda and Lesley, my agents and friends; Claire Ferguson, friend and author, thank you for all your help with sourcing difficult equipment issues!

Below are the chefs and food writers who have graciously contributed to this book. I am in awe of their talent and knowledge and can not thank them enough for sharing their passion and their wonderful recipes.

PUBLISHER: We would like to thank the following for contributing recipes to this book (*in order of appearance*):
Giorgio Locatelli (proprietor *Locanda Locatelli* restaurant, London),
Jean Claude Guillon, Luis Irizar (of the Escuela de Cocina Luis Irizar, San Sebastian, Spain), Mariá José Sevilla, Daniel Boulud, Todd English, Roger Vergé, Sophie Grigson, Polycarpos Demetriou, Huseyin Ozer, Anissa Helou, Greg Malouf, Paula Wolfert, Claudia Roden, Boujemma Mars (executive chef Mamounia Hotel, Marakesh, Morocco), Joyce Goldstein.
All guest recipes are used with permission.

index